JOURNEY TO FREEDOM

Growing Up TO BE *President*

Mary Carol Ghislin

Cover Photo Credit:

Focused Adventures;

(John Adams, 1793) National Portrait Gallery, Smithsonian Institution;

(Washington, 1783) National Portrait Gallery, Smithsonian Institution; gift of Katie Louchheim;

(Madison, c. 1801) National Portrait Gallery, Smithsonian Institution;

(Jefferson, 1786) National Portrait Gallery, Smithsonian Institution; bequest of Charles Francis Adams;

(c. 1818, Monroe) Smithsonian American Art Museum, Bequest of Mary Elizabeth Spencer

Cover and Book design by
Eric Dossou and Armando Lopez

Table of Contents

Preface

The information about each President in this book is selected based on historians' discussions about the major accomplishments or failures of each man. These topics are always subject to change as new research comes to light through the decades. Particularly, the concept of "Founding Fathers" has been re-examined.

The label can simultaneously convey admiration or offend by exclusion. Yet the term has not been abandoned. Women historians rightly point out that several colonial women were influential in the founding of the country. Often named are Abigail Adams, Dolly Madison, and Mercy Otis Warren. Each had a prominent husband and were influential in the early development of committees of correspondence, the constitution, and the organization of the White House. Moreover, Warren wrote and published the first account of the Revolution.

Yet no historian dismisses the idea of a founding group whose tireless work for the young republic deserves recognition, acclaim, and their country's gratitude. In this volume, the labeling of the first five presidents as Founding Fathers is in no way intended to imply that they are the only persons deserving of the title.

"Signing of the Declaration of Independence," by John Trumbull, 1817

A Broader Group of Founding Fathers

In addition to the three women named above, the following additional men are also considered by many historians to be Founding Fathers, though they were never presidents:

- Samuel Adams was John Adams' cousin and a founding member of the first Committee of Correspondence in Massachusetts.

- Benjamin Franklin served as an ambassador to France during the American Revolution. He also organized a militia in Pennsylvania, was clerk to the Pennsylvania legislature, and became deputy postmaster general for all the northern colonies.

- Alexander Hamilton was the first secretary of the treasury and established the foundation for the federal banking system.

- Patrick Henry became a successful lawyer and legislator. He was famous for his speeches that strongly defended liberty.

- John Jay was appointed the first chief justice of the United States and president of the Continental Congress.

- John Marshall founded the U.S. system of constitutional law and established the practice of judicial review.

George Mason wrote an early declaration of individual rights as a founding member of the Virginia Committee of Safety. In it, he vehemently opposed slavery. Thomas Jefferson knew of his work, and it influenced the writing of the Declaration of Independence.

One could also add Paul Revere, Thomas Paine, and others to this list above. In addition to the Founding Fathers category, labels such as Jacksonian Democracy and Forgettable Presidents are now also discussed among historians in the light of new opinions. Yet none of these new points-of-view should deter the study of the forty-five men, thus far, who rose to those leadership positions. As the award-winning historian David McCullough once said, we should come to know them as human beings, flawed, yet aspiring to great deeds. For if they were gods, they would not deserve to be recognized for the good that they did.

Mary Carol Ghislin

George Washington

Facing Misfortune in Childhood

Rule no. 22 "Show not yourself glad at the Misfortune of another though he were your enemy."

From, *Youth[']s Behaviour, or Decency in Conversation Amongst Men*

Young George Washington knew misfortune well. When he was eleven, his father died suddenly, leaving him without the funds for an education in England, as his older brothers had received. The Washingtons were part of the upper class of landowners in Virginia. Being situated just under the aristocracy, the social customs of the day demanded that George would get a university education.

1st President of the United States, Founding Father

He would have learned Latin and read all the classic Greek and Latin texts in philosophy, political science, and literature. He was expected to learn other languages as well, like French or German. But after his father's death, he received only instruction from a local school, learning mathematics, reading, and writing.

Following Guidance from Family

While his older brothers were ready to be accepted into the upper classes, George was suddenly left out. Recognizing George's need, his older brother Lawrence with his father-in-law and aristocratic neighbor, Colonel William Fairfax, took him under their wing. They guided him toward a career as a land surveyor and in the military.

At about the age of 14 and guided by Colonel Fairfax, he copied geometry problems from *The Compleat Surveyor*, a popular school text. He learned the science and geometry of land surveying, or indirect measurement, preparing him to legally mark the boundaries of individual properties. At 17, he began his first surveying job. Within a few years, he had surveyed 60,000 acres owned by Colonel Fairfax and other acquaintances, including Lt. Governor Robert Dinwiddie.

Adopting Social Manners and Customs

Perhaps because George was concerned about his social station, he also copied all 110 rules of civility from the social manners book, *Youth[']s Behavior*. The rules covered formal events, friendly encounters, and everyday courtesies. From this study, and perhaps also from his own misfortune, he acquired a sense of honor and consideration of those about him.

At 19, George traveled with Lawrence to Barbados, southeast of Puerto Rico in the Caribbean Sea. Likely through his connection to Colonel Fairfax, he toured the British military installations and dined with high-ranking military commanders. He began to imagine a military career. Yet misfortune struck again, and he contracted smallpox. His only remark in his journal was, "Strongly attacked with the smallpox." It was his last journal entry for the next twenty-four days.

The Barbados journey was a gateway from his country childhood into the larger world of military life and government. In Barbados, he was treated as a gentleman, and visited Bridgetown, the largest city he had ever seen. Moreover, the sobering experience of survival from the most serious illness of his life launched George into a new maturity. Upon his return, the Virginia Governor called him a young "person of distinction."

"Washington the Young Surveyor," by Henry Wolf, c. 1888

Joining the Military

In 1753 at age 21, he joined the Virginia militia. His first mission was a winter's journey deep into the Ohio Country to bring a written challenge to the French. He served with distinction on that mission and was rewarded with a promotion to Lt. Colonel. Until 1758, he fought for the British in the French and Indian War, when he resigned his commission in 1759.

Leaving the military behind, he and his wife settled onto his estate on Mount Vernon, and he farmed and served in the Virginia colonial government. On June 15, 1775, the Second Continental Congress met in Philadelphia. George Washington attended as a representative from Virginia. The Congress' main order of business was to appoint a commander-in-chief of the Continental Army fighting the Revolution. Washington was unanimously elected.

Persisting in the Face of Defeat

Whereafter, he immediately rode to Massachusetts and took charge of the army. The early battles were resounding defeats for Washington's troops. They were compelled into one retreat after another, from Boston all the way south to the Delaware River in Pennsylvania.

On the bitterest of winter nights, with most of his army only days away from the end of their enlistment, Washington crossed the Delaware to attack the enemy stationed at Trenton, New Jersey. It was a morale-boosting victory. Another march north to engage the enemy at Princeton left the colonial troops triumphant. Those two victories, and ten dollars in pay for each soldier who agreed to re-enlist, kept the army intact.

But they suffered two more defeats before they finally arrived at Valley Forge (1777) for their winter quarters. Lacking food, clothing, shoes, and shelter, Washington sent younger generals out to scour the countryside for food. He directed the troops to build rude shelters and search the area for straw as flooring. He spent the winter writing to Congress demanding more supplies and defending himself against charges of incompetence. All while directing the officers to continue to train and drill the soldiers.

President Washington posed in this uniform for portraits after the war.

Setting Examples

It would be four more years before the Continental Army defeated the British at Yorktown in 1781. Then in 1783, Washington resigned his commission, in keeping with his belief that the military was a servant to a civil government. Relieved, he went home to Mount Vernon where he had longed for his life as a country gentleman.

The new states struggled through six years trying to govern. As much as Washington yearned for a quiet country life, he recognized the country's difficulties. So, he volunteered to help develop a stronger constitution.

Taking the First Presidency

In 1788, the new government voted unanimously for George Washington to be the country's first President. On April 30, 1789, he took the oath of office and began a difficult period, struggling to keep the country unified. He knew that every decision would be an example for generations, and he felt the weight of that responsibility.

- He traveled across the southern states between March 21 and June 4, 1791 to encourage unity. Crowds greeted him wherever he went. He met with indigenous peoples' chiefs who inquired about their treaties. He also met with the Georgia governor to discuss problems with Spanish Florida, who would not return runaway enslaved Africans.

- In establishing his Cabinet, he chose men based on merit, quitting the traditional European method of appointment through social rank.

- Even though the word "cabinet" does not appear in the Constitution, Washington selected trusted men to advise him. He based this on the practice of war councils

"Mount Vernon," by Frances Mary "Jennie" Bellows Millard, c. 1850

he used during the Revolution. This administrative structure remains to this day.

- After two terms in office, he decided not to seek a third term. Thus, he was the first person in the world to set the precedent for a peaceful transfer of power.

- In putting down the whiskey rebellion (an anti-tax rebellion in western Pennsylvania), he established the right of the federal government to levy taxes.*

The Presidential Footprint

Although President George Washington could be cited for many of his accomplishments, one consistent quality that was the basis of all his action was his devotion to civic duty. He repeatedly accepted the call to aid his government when he often preferred the life of a country gentleman.

*For comprehension and vocabulary work, as well as a mini-lesson on freedom of religion, see the *Discussion Guide,* pages 2–4.

Birth: February 22, 1732   **Place:** Pope's Creek, Virginia   **Occuption:** Soldier, Planter

Religion: Anglican   **Term of Office:** 1789 to 1797   **Death:** December 14, 1799

Position on Slavery: Washington inherited 11 enslaved Africans from his father's estate.

- Martha brought 84 enslaved people to the marriage as part of her marriage "dower share."

- Washington purchased at least 65 men, women, and children between 1750 and 1770.

- In his will, he emancipated the 120 individuals that he owned outright. This did not include the people that Martha Custis had brought into the marriage.

John Adams

Inheriting a Dream

John Adams descended from John Alden, a crew member aboard the Mayflower. John Alden married Priscilla Mullins, the daughter of one of the investors in the voyage, who also traveled on the Mayflower with his entire family. John and Priscilla married in 1623 and had ten children, most of whom stayed in the immediate area for decades to come. Their descendant, John Adams, was born in Quincy, Massachusetts only 110 years later. His parents were Deacon John Adams and Susanna, farmers and active members of their local Congregational Church, the name of the Puritans' church.

2nd President of the United States, Founding Father

Choosing His Path

Young John worked with his father on their farm. They worked well together, and his father decided that because John seemed so bright, he should attend the university to study law. Yet one day after school, John told his father he had no interest in college. He only wanted to be a farmer. The next day his father kept him by his side and worked him hard all day. At the end of the ordeal, he asked his son whether he still liked farming. To which young John replied, "I like it very well, sir."

Frustrated, his father questioned further until John admitted that he did not like his teacher. His father immediately withdrew him from that school and enrolled him in a private school under a schoolmaster named John Marsh. Finally, young Adams' interest sparked, and he took up his studies with vigor. He grew particularly fond of Cicero's orations, a collection of speeches made by a famous Roman lawyer and speaker, which supported John's developing views on government.

At age 15, he enrolled in Harvard under a partial scholarship, and his father sold ten acres of land to pay for the rest. Young John learned Latin and studied science and mathematics. It is said that he was never seen without a book in his hand.

The birthplace of John Adams and John Quincy Adams

Committing to Self-Improvement

During the first few months of teaching in an isolated country school, he contracted to read law with an attorney in Worcester for two years. In those days, training in the law was done with a practicing lawyer. There were no law schools to go to. So, John taught in the little country school and read law simultaneously, until he moved back to Braintree to set up his own law practice. He continued to study law on his own and visited court to watch lawyers argue cases.

In 1759, he was admitted to the bar and took his first case. He lost and was humiliated. But he determined to study harder and turned to Cicero for inspiration: "The first way for a man to set himself on the road to glorious reputation is to win renown."

He took Cicero's advice and moved to Boston where more cases were available that might provide him more possibilities to develop a "glorious reputation." But he was very self-conscious about his shortcomings. With help from friends, he closely watched people he admired and compared his behavior to theirs to improve himself and become a polished lawyer.

Developing a Glorious Reputation

It took him three years to win his first case, and by 1770 he was the busiest lawyer in Boston. His reputation was established. He wrote opinion pieces for the newspapers, and he was chosen to defend the British soldiers involved in the Boston Massacre, a riot between British soldiers and colonists in which several colonists were killed. Even with emotions running high across the city, he won that case by proving that the soldiers had been provoked by the mob and were defending themselves.

- In 1774, he was selected as one of four Massachusetts delegates to the First Continental Congress, where his reputation as a plain-speaking rebel grew. His self-confidence had matured to a point where many people thought he was arrogant. Yet, he argued passionately for independence and evolved into one of the leaders of that movement.

- One year later, he was serving in the Second Continental Congress when war broke out against England, and he nominated George Washington to serve as Commander-in-Chief of the Continental Army.

Drawing depicting the Boston Massacre.

- He served on ninety committees and chaired twenty of them.

- He worked with Thomas Jefferson and Benjamin Franklin on the Declaration of Independence.

- He traveled to Europe to open avenues of trade for the new country and became its first Minister to England. He traveled so extensively that at one point he had not seen his wife or children in five years.

Seal used by John Adams to sign the peace treaty that ended the revolutionary war

Taking the Oath of Office

When Adams took the oath of office for the Presidency in 1797, he inherited foreign policy problems from a new war between Britain and France.

Caught between Britain and France, the United States struggled to maintain neutrality. Although President Washington had repaired the United States' relationship with Britain, the relationship between America and France became worse during Adams' term.

France began seizing American ships on the suspicion that they were aligned with Great Britain. When President Adams sent diplomats to France to work out the problems, the French government demanded a $10 million loan for the country before they would negotiate a peace treaty. Americans became so angry that Adams acted quickly, requesting Congress to provide funds for his plan to improve Americans' defense:

- He wanted to boost the Navy.

- He wanted to create a provisional army and the authority to call 80,000 men to active duty.

- In response, Congress created the Navy Department and organized the Marine Corps.

- They also passed the Alien and Sedition Acts. These laws raised the residency requirement for citizenship from 5 to 14 years. They gave the President broad powers to deport "aliens" during wartime and made it illegal to "print, utter, or publish...any false, scandalous, and malicious writing" about the government.

- The law was pointedly aimed at the Democrat-Republicans and supported the Federalists, which was John Adams' party.

In effect, President Adams paraded a show of force to get France to the negotiating table. It worked. By the winter of 1799, France agreed to talk. But the Alien and

Sedition Acts, which had been largely aimed at Adams' opposing party, the Democratic-Republicans, caused a backlash. It was the first test of the country's commitment to free speech. Partly due to these laws, John Adams lost his bid for re-election.*

The Presidential Footprint

Historians have criticized Adams for signing the Alien and Sedition Acts, though some point out that he never implemented them. Moreover, he embodied leniency in forgiving many Americans involved in tax rebellions. Overall, historians accept John Adams' term of office as one governed by morality, compassion, and the rule of law.

*For comprehension and vocabulary work, as well as a mini-lesson on John Adams and King George, see the *Discussion Guide*, pages 5–7.

Birth: October 30, 1735   **Place:** Braintree, Massachusetts   **Occupation:** Lawyer

Religion: Unitarian   **Term of Office:** 1797 to 1801   **Death:** July 4, 1826

Position on Slavery: John Adams owned no enslaved persons.

- His wife Abigail hired white servants and free African servants.

- Abigail may also have rented enslaved Africans from neighbors and paid their enslavers for work in the Vice President's and President's houses.

Thomas Jefferson

Living the Planter's Life

Thomas Jefferson was born into a planter family, who relied on the use of enslaved people to support their lifestyle. Though they were not among the wealthiest Virginians, they lived a comfortable life. His earliest memory was at three years old, being carried on horseback by an enslaved man, as the family moved to a wilderness area that his father was managing. From age 3 to 9, young Thomas was free to explore the Virginia wilderness and read books.

3rd President of the United States, Founding Father

At nine years of age, he entered his so-called "formal" studies, meaning that he lived with his teacher for nine months out of every year. This arrangement continued until he enrolled in the College of William and Mary at age 16, where he studied rhetoric, or the methods of formal argumentation. He was also a serious student of science, mathematics, philosophy, and literature. After college, he read law with one of the most respected lawyers in the colonies. At the time, law schools did not exist. Instead, young men studied as an apprentice under an established lawyer. After five years studying, Jefferson was admitted to the Virginia bar in 1767.

Living a Country Lawyer's Life

In his early career, he was a country lawyer on a circuit, which meant that he followed traveling judges to the towns where they held court. He was not a great trial lawyer. As many observers thought his mannerisms in court were somewhat shy. Yet he gained a powerful reputation as a legal scholar, as his writings in the coming revolutionary period would prove the point.

It was during these early travels that he met Martha Wayles Skelton and married her on January 1, 1772. They moved into a small one-room brick house while Thomas began building their permanent home. He called it Monticello, which means "little mountain" because it was built on top of a small hill on his property.

Organizing and Describing the Revolution

In the early years of his married life, Thomas became a member of the Virginia House of Burgesses, the lower legislative house of congress, like the House of Representatives. During his term there, he organized the Virginia Committee of Correspondence. These correspondence committees were underground supporters of independence and played a key role in the revolution. They set up a secret system of communication between the states to spread information about potential independence from England.

During his time on this committee, Jefferson wrote an early version of his political ideas. It was called "Summary View of the Rights of British America." Someone published it beyond the scope of the committee without his consent. Yet the ideas caught fire, inciting great public admiration. He later stood with Patrick Henry as one of the great articulators of the desire for independence.

The desk that Jefferson wrote the Declaration of Independence on

Writing the Declaration of Independence

In 1776, Jefferson was in Philadelphia as a member of the Second Continental Congress where he was assigned to the committee that would draft a national statement of independence. The members of the committee turned to Jefferson for the major portion of writing. After the larger congress debated the contents and made several changes, it was adopted on July 4. They called it "The Unanimous Declaration of the 13 United States of America." It was the single most important piece of writing that Jefferson ever produced, and it secured his place among the greatest of the Founding Fathers.

Writing the Law for Religious Freedom

During the Revolutionary War, from 1776 to 1779 Jefferson served in the Virginia House of Delegates sponsoring legislation based on his ideals. He was most proud of passing the Virginia Bill for Establishing Religious Freedom, which passed in 1786, only about 3 years after the Revolutionary War ended. It was the first American statement of the separation of church and state. It also was the first law to state that men

Engraving of Jefferson writing the Declaration of Independence

had a right to their own opinions about religion. The law deeply influenced a similar law in the Bill of Rights, which was passed in 1791.

Taking the Oath of the Presidency

On March 4, 1801 Thomas Jefferson took the oath of office for President of the United States. He believed in a smaller, weaker federal government. To that end, he cut back on the 316 jobs that were subject to his appointment. He also reduced the size of the army and navy.

Yet, foreign affairs pulled Jefferson's attention to duties that forced him to take actions that characterized a strong, central government. One problem that presented itself was the news that Spain had given all its territory of Louisiana to France.

Although Jefferson was friendly to France, there were two circumstances that caused him concern. The first was that Spain had at one time closed the Mississippi River to American travel. The potential for this happening again seemed to be an event to prevent at all costs. And the second was that with Napoleon now the leader of France and revealing a long-held desire to be an Emperor, Jefferson worried that sharing a border with France would not be helpful to Americans.

Jefferson was concerned that American farmers could lose their access to the port of New Orleans. So, he sent ambassadors to France to negotiate the purchase of

Map of the Louisiana purchase

New Orleans. The ambassadors were surprised to learn that, in fact, Napoleon was looking for a way to finance a new war in Europe. Because of this, he was eager to sell nearly all of France's land. So the young United States bought 828,000 acres, at $0.04 per acre. The total for this Louisiana Purchase, as it came to be called, was $15 million.

Jefferson immediately commissioned a party of twenty-eight explorers to travel the lands, called The Lewis and Clark Expedition, and report back. They took two and a half years to traverse the territory.*

The Presidential Footprint

President Jefferson, perhaps more than any other Founding Father, has received a large share of criticism. For, having written the most eloquent statement of freedom to that point in history, he nevertheless relied on enslaved labor.

One might say that his legacy is best stated in his own description of the balance between the individual and his nation. In Jefferson's inaugural address, he said the American government was, at the time, the only one on earth "where every man, at the call of the law, would fly to the standard of the law, and would meet invasions of the public order as his own personal concern." The way to balance individual freedom and national need was, according to Jefferson, a matter of loyalty to the rule of law.

Statue of Lewis and Clark

*For comprehension and vocabulary work, as well as a mini-lesson on Jefferson's letter to Meriwether Lewis, see the *Discussion Guide*, pages 8–10.

Birth: April 13, 1743

Place: Shadwell plantation, Goochland County, Virginia

Occupation: Lawyer, Planter

Religion: No affiliation

Term of Office: 1801 to 1809

Death: July 4, 1826

Position on Slavery: He owned and profited from about 600 enslaved persons during his lifetime.

- He was rumored to have had children with enslaved housemaid Sally Hemmings.
- A formal committee concluded in the year 2000 that this rumor was likely to be true.
- Jefferson freed all of Sally Hemmings' children in his will. He freed no other enslaved individuals on his plantation.
- Jefferson did not free Sally Hemmings.

James Madison

Suffering from Great Fear

James Madison was raised on a Virginia plantation, the oldest of twelve children, only seven of whom survived to adulthood. He grew up during the French and Indian War which began when he was 3 and lasted until he was 12 and recalled suffering from great fear of an Indian attack. As a result of this fear, he was a sickly and small child who suffered from stress-induced seizures. He stayed close to his mother, supported by seven loving siblings, and read books.

4th President of the United States, Founding Father

Focusing His Studies in College and Beyond

He learned Greek and Latin from private tutors, then went on to enroll in college. He graduated in 1771 from the College of New Jersey, later called Princeton University, in only 2 years. But he stayed to study Hebrew and philosophy. He studied law after he graduated but found that he was not really interested in it.

In 1772, he entered public service when he joined the local Committee of Safety. It was a small, private group that established letter-writing communication between the colonies. They kept people informed of the issues that were fostering the growing call for independence from England.

Polishing a Quiet Persistence

In 1776, he attended the Virginia Convention where they debated independence. He was soft-spoken, even shy, and was only 5' 4", yet his persistence in arguing a political point stood in stark contrast to his physical demeanor. In a regular election for state delegates to the new general assembly, he lost to a more extroverted candidate. But his growing friendship with Governor Thomas Jefferson led to an appointment to the Virginia Council of State, which governed the state during the Revolutionary War. The two men continued to develop their friendship, which remained close for the rest of Jefferson's life.

Page of the Articles of Confederation, the United States' first unsuccessful constitution

Although James lacked commanding public speaking skills, at 29, he became the youngest member of the Continental Congress. Although he was shy, he spent so many hours preparing for meetings that he made impressive contributions to every discussion.

Cultivating His Concept of Government

When Congress called for a Constitutional Convention in 1787, James spent months in preparation developing a document he called the Virginia Plan. It was an early conceptualization of what became the Constitution of the United States. While the Convention originally only intended to revise their weak Articles of Confederation, Madison lobbied tirelessly for his vision of a stronger, centralized government. He envisioned it as having three branches, each independent of the other, but with powers that could check the functions of the other two.

His calm persistence won, and the Convention adopted his ideas, which were then sent to the states for ratification. While the states debated, Madison wrote essays for the newspapers that explained how the Constitution worked and the theories behind it. Alexander Hamilton and John Jay also wrote some essays, and the collection became known as the Federalist Papers, the most comprehensive statement of American political theory in existence.

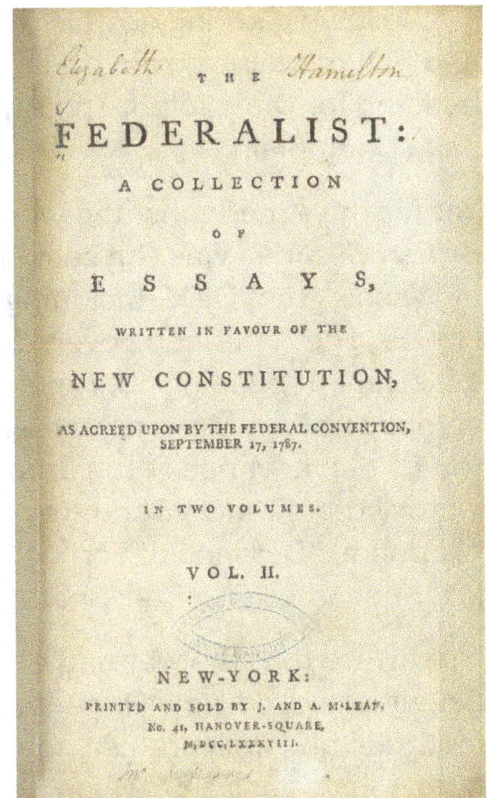

Title page for a bound copy of the Federalist Papers

In 1789, as a member of the House of Representatives, he lobbied for the passage of the Bill of Rights. As his reputation grew, President Jefferson appointed James Madison to be his Secretary of State.

Taking the Presidential Oath of Office

In 1808, he was elected President, America's fourth. As was Adams and Jefferson, Madison was swamped by foreign policy difficulties. The war between Britain and France had made the high seas dangerous for American ships because each warring party blamed the United States for siding with the enemy. When Madison took office, the United States and France had already resumed trade, but Great Britain continued to threaten both French and U.S. ships.

Fighting the War of 1812

Finally, Madison went to Congress to declare war against Britain with the following complaints: 1. Continued British attacks on American ships; 2. British arming of Indians against American settlers; 3. Trade restrictions against American goods. In two weeks, Congress approved a war against Great Britain.

During the War of 1812, Americans suffered early defeats in Canada and the Northwest Territory (Michigan, Wisconsin, Illinois, and Ohio). President Madison and his generals responded months later with resounding victories in York (now Toronto). The Americans burned the British government buildings in York and then pushed toward victories against British holdings in Alabama.

The following spring, Britain attacked in the Northeast and occupied American ports and half of Maine. From that advantage, the British swept down through New York, heading for the capital. The American troops rallied and stopped them in a battle on Lake Champlain.

Yet for the Americans, the worst of the British victories was the sacking and burning of Washington, D.C.—including the White House. The American government fled while government buildings burned. It was the soldiers at Fort McHenry who finally stopped the British advance in the area. This was the victory that Francis Scott Key celebrated in his poem, "Defence of Fort M'Henry" which later became "The Star-Spangled Banner."

The Capture of Washington. Cundee, J., Publisher

Not aware that the war had officially ended, Britain attacked New Orleans, but American forces answered with resounding fortitude and delivered an coup de grace to the British. This victory buoyed President Madison's popularity, which had been suffering after the burning of the White House.*

The Presidential Footprint

President Madison did not have a physical stature, like Washington and Jefferson, that dominated a room. Yet historians have labeled Madison a "master" of the so-called "small arena." His quiet intellect was a formidable opponent in an argument, earning him the well-deserved title "Father of the Constitution." Some historians have

Painting of the Battle of New Orleans. Kurz & Allison. ca, 1890

noted that were it not for this achievement, the shame of being chased out of the White House as the British set fire to it, might have driven his legacy into oblivion.

However, in recent years, some historians have equated Madison's handling of The War of 1812 with Lincoln's leadership during The Civil War. In fact, at a time when Great Britain challenged the legitimacy of our existence, Madison stood firm. When they invaded the Northeast and occupied our ports, many in New England organized to secede from the new union with a plan to rejoin the British Empire. Just like Lincoln was destined to do forty-eight years later, Madison held the union together, and this secessionist movement faded into the mists of history. The War of 1812 became unofficially called the Second American Revolution.

*For comprehension and vocabulary work, as well as mini-lessons on checks and balances and The War of 1812, see the *Discussion Guide*, pages 11-12, and 22.

Birth: March 16, 1751   **Place:** Port Conway, Virginia   **Occupation:** Politician, Planter

Religion: Episcopalian   **Term of Office:** 1809 to 1817   **Death:** June 28, 1836

Position on Slavery: He inherited more than 100 enslaved people from his father.

- He brought some enslaved staff with him to Washington, D. C.

- He also "rented" other enslaved staff from permanent Washington households, a common practice of the day.

- Madison was known to avoid excessive cruelty to his enslaved staff, fearing a revolt.

- He purchased White House staff member John Freeman from Thomas Jefferson, so that Freeman could stay in Washington with his family. Madison freed him in 1815, and the Freeman family became some of the earliest freed Black Americans in Washington.

- Madison did not free any of the enslaved individuals on his personal estate in his will.

James Monroe

Facing Misfortune Early in Life

James was in his teens his father died, leaving him and his two brothers orphaned. His mother had died long before. So, an uncle stepped in and mentored the three boys. In 1774 at age sixteen, he enrolled in the College of William and Mary, which was in Williamsburg, the capital of Virginia at the time.

Immediately, James aligned himself with the revolutionary cause which was reaching a high-pitched fervor in Williamsburg. In fact, the British governor had already fled with his family, fearing that the town was an unsafe environment. Without hesitation, James joined a group of young men who shortly thereafter raided the arsenal, stealing 200 muskets and 300 swords for the revolution.

5th President of the United States, Founding Father

Joining the Revolutionary Cause

By 1776, James joined the Virginia militia and soon became an officer in the Continental Army. He fought under General George Washington in several major battles, suffering a severe wound in the battle of Trenton. Although he achieved the rank of major, an oversupply of officers made it impossible for him to receive his own command.

So, he returned to the Virginia militia where the opportunities were greater. By 1779, he reached the rank of colonel, and Governor Thomas Jefferson sent him on a mission to discover the location of the British. After the war, the ambitious young Monroe requested that Thomas Jefferson train him in the study of law.

Setting Out for a Life in Politics

Having declared his politics early in life, Monroe never wavered in his dedication and ran for election to the Virginia Assembly in 1782, the same year that he passed the bar exam. He won a seat and was appointed to the Council of State, whose members advised the governor.

Only one year later, he was elected to the Continental Congress at age 25. During his term, he focused on securing American rights to the Mississippi River and developing government for Americans' push to the western lands.

Revealing an Independent Spirit

After only one year in Congress, he married and returned to Fredericksburg, Virginia to establish a home and practice law. He wasn't finished with his government career though.

- He attended the Virginia U.S. Constitution ratification convention, where he voted against ratifying.

- Leading this independent faction, he campaigned for a constitution with direct election of the President by the people, and a strong bill of rights.

- After the Constitution passed, he ran against James Madison for a seat in Congress and lost.

Accepting Every Appointment

- Many historians think that James Monroe was the most qualified person ever to be President. After his loss to James Madison, he continued in politics holding several offices.

- He was appointed to the U.S. Senate in 1790.

- He worked closely with Thomas Jefferson and James Madison to oppose the establishment of a strong central government.

- In 1794, President Washington appointed him Minister to France. Washington blamed him for the deteriorating relationship with France and recalled him in 1796.

- In 1799, he was elected Governor of Virginia and worked with Thomas Jefferson to set up public education.

- In 1803, he went to France to negotiate the Louisiana Purchase.

- He was Secretary of State and Secretary of War at the same time.

  - In 1811, he was elected Governor of Virginia, although President Madison appointed him Secretary of State in that same year.

  - During the War of 1812, the Secretary of War resigned, and Monroe stepped into the job, as the British advanced on Washington.

  - Monroe stayed in the city to help evacuate it. He returned after the British burned it, and Madison put him in charge of the city's defense.

Ushering in the Era of Good Feelings

In 1817 President Monroe toured the country. Upon arriving in Boston, he was introduced with a pronouncement that the country was entering an "Era of Good Feelings." After their second victory against the British in the War of 1812, Americans were developing a nationalist feeling that supported a strong centralized government.

Yet, the danger of sectionalism was beginning to show. To acknowledge regional needs, Monroe chose advisors from the North, the South, and

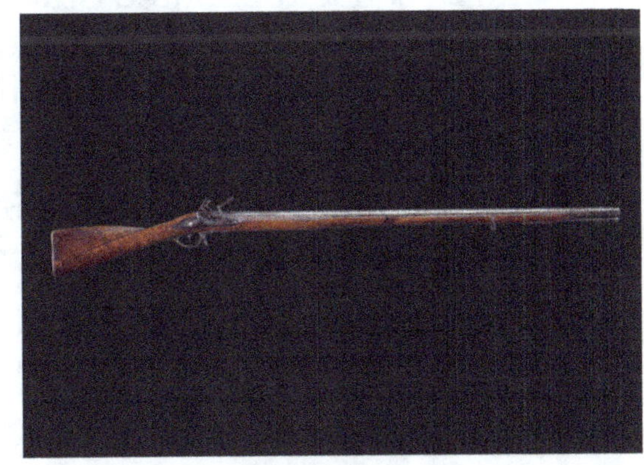

Musket from circa 1770

the West (although his Western candidate refused the appointment). His cabinet was strong, filled with men of good character, solid education, experience, and excellent management skills.

Testing the Era of Good Feelings

With the application of Missouri to the United States, the bitter arguments over enslaved versus free statehood began. They were to haunt the nation for the next forty years. Yet, in the moment, President Monroe showed remarkable mediation skills. He decided that it would be unconstitutional to put restrictions on one state. So, he encouraged a compromise.

Both Maine and Missouri applied for statehood at about the same time—Maine as a free state, and Missouri as a state that wanted to allow enslaved status. Because many in Congress feared that slavery would continue throughout the new Western states to come, they wanted to stop slavery's advance into those territories.

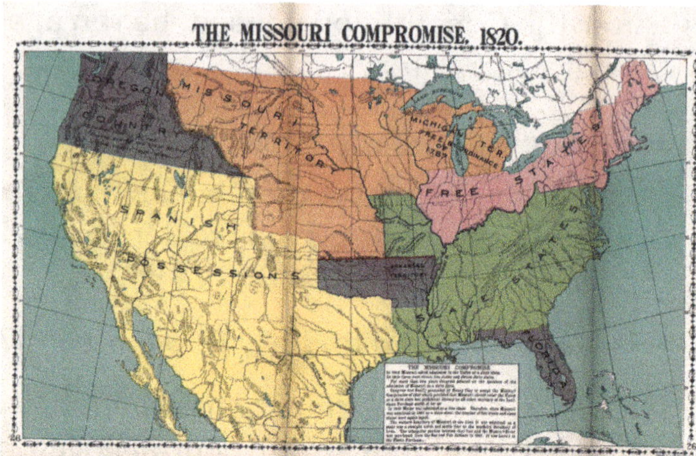

Map shows the results of the Missouri Compromise, which allowed Missouri into the union as a slave state

- The Missouri Compromise allowed enslaved status only in Missouri, but in no other state north of Missouri's southern borderline.

- The Compromise also forbade the Missouri legislature from doing anything in the future that would curtail citizen's rights, including mixed-race citizens and the formerly enslaved black population.

- The Missouri state legislature agreed to these rules, and Missouri was admitted to the Union in 1821.*

Taking a Stand Against European Colonialism

During the early 1800s, many Spanish colonies in the Americas had obtained their freedom. Because the United States felt a kinship with their struggles against foreign domination, President Monroe developed a foreign policy statement to protect the Western Hemisphere from further interference. In 1823 he made a speech to Congress.

- He announced that the United States would maintain a neutral status in all European conflicts.

- He warned European nations that the U.S. would not stand by if they tried to reclaim any former colonies.

- He proclaimed that the U.S. would not accept any new colonization by any European country in the Americas.

By the 1850s, Congress began calling this declaration the Monroe Doctrine. It remained the foundation of American policy toward Central and South America for the rest of the nineteenth century and throughout the twentieth century.

The Presidential Footprint

As the last of the so-called "Virginia dynasty" presidents, President James Monroe was notable for his intellect and ability to work with people. He is credited with excellent negotiation and management skills, particularly in navigating the dangerous waters of the Missouri Compromise. His Monroe Doctrine was the United States' first foreign-policy declaration. It became a signal to Europe that the United States was here to stay and that it was to be taken as a leader in the post-colonial world yet to come.

*For comprehension and vocabulary work, as well as mini-lessons on the Missouri Compromise and sectionalism, see the *Discussion Guide*, pages 13-14.

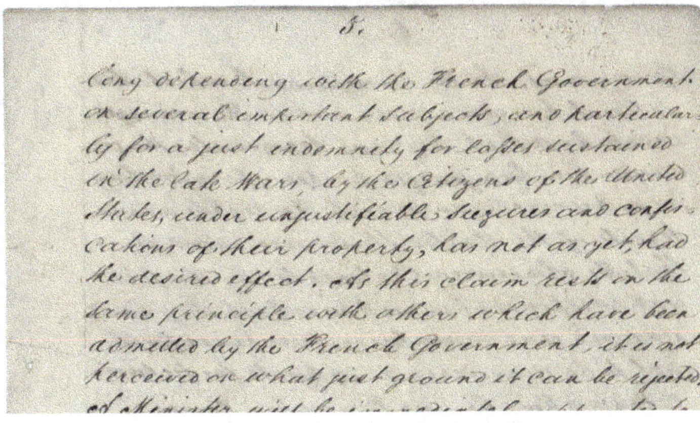

First page of the speech that became the Monroe Doctrine

Birth: April 28, 1758

Religion: Episcopalian

Place: Westmoreland County, Virginia

Term of Office: 1817 to 1825

Occupation: Lawyer

Death: July 4, 1831

Position on Slavery: James Monroe inherited his parents' land and enslaved people.

- While Governor of Virginia, Monroe faced the worst slave revolt in U.S. history on August 30, 1800.

- Receiving word that an armed revolt was imminent, Governor Monroe ordered the Virginia militia to patrol Richmond streets.

- For two days, they searched enslaved families' homes arresting over seventy people. Eight were sold into the deep South; twenty-five acquitted; and thirteen were pardoned. Twenty-six were executed.

- The 1810 census shows forty-nine enslaved individuals living on the Monroe property.

- Monroe had at least three enslaved women and four enslaved men serving him at the White House.

plant. In the afternoon I passed by a field in which several poor slaves had lately been executed, on the charge of having an intention to rise against their masters. A lawyer who was present at their trials at Richmond, informed me that on one of them being asked, what he had to say to the court on his defence, he replied, in a manly tone of voice: "I have nothing more to offer than what General Washington would have had to offer, had he been taken by the British and put to trial by them. I have adventured my life in endeavouring to obtain the liberty of my countrymen, and am a willing sacrifice in their cause: and I beg, as a favour, that I may be immediately led to execution. I know that you have pre-determined to shed my blood, why then all this mockery of a trial?"

Account of an enslaved man on trial for leading an uprising

Founding Fathers Who Were Not Presidents

John Jay wrote several of the Federalist Papers (with Alexander Hamilton and James Madison) to persuade the states to approve the Constitution.

Benjamin Franklin served as an Ambassador to France during the revolution. He organized a militia in Pennsylvania, was clerk to the Pennsylvania legislature, and became the deputy postmaster general for all the northern colonies.

John Quincy Adams, Abigail's son and the 6th President, recalled that he used to watch his mother melt pewter and make bullets for the war effort with this mold.

Abigail Adams once famously reminded her husband, who was at the constitutional convention, to "remember the ladies" as they finalized the Constitution.

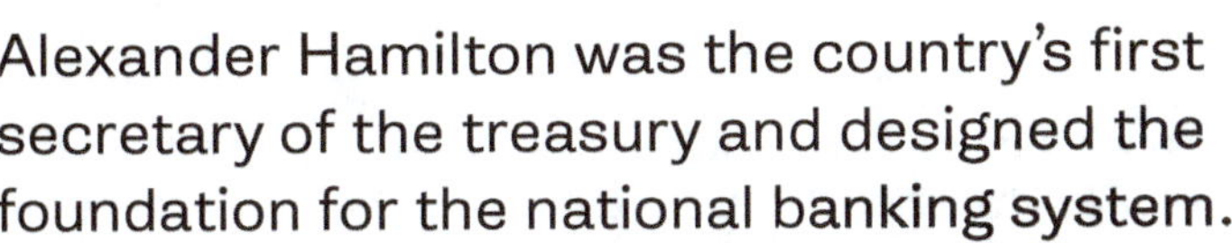

Samuel Adams was John Adams' cousin and served as Governor of Massachusetts. Samuel was also instrumental in establishing some of the earliest committees of correspondence.

Alexander Hamilton was the country's first secretary of the treasury and designed the foundation for the national banking system.

John Quincy Adams

Fearing for His Life

John Quincy Adams' early memories were filled with fear for his life. His father, John Adams (2nd president), was off leading the Revolutionary War through his work with the Continental Congress. For eight-year-old John Quincy, the Revolutionary War raged close to his home. He and his mother witnessed the Battle of Bunker Hill, watching from a nearby hillside. Soldiers were regularly marching through his hometown while the booming cannon fire hovered as a deadly threat. Since his father was more absent than present, his mother taught him reading, writing, and mathematics. Both his parents were avid readers of the classics, which they dutifully assigned to young John Quincy. Thus, he was schooled in the traditional English gentlemanly manners.

6th President of the United States

Traveling through the World

After the war, his father took him overseas with him. At only ten years of age, he went to Paris while his father negotiated treaties. He and his brother Charles attended school in Paris with Benjamin Franklin's grandsons.

For seven years, John Quincy traveled around Europe with his father. As well as in Paris, they had extended stays in St. Petersburg and Amsterdam, and his father's envoy duties also took them on business trips to Spain, England, Prussia, and Sweden. John Quincy was not just tagging along on these trips. In St. Petersburg, at only fourteen years old, he served as a translator for the American ambassador.

Returning Home

He was only seventeen when he returned to the United States. He enrolled in Harvard and finished his studies in only two years and then went to law school. In 1803, he was appointed Senator to Congress for the state of Massachusetts. He was not popular in the Senate and lost his seat after only one term. All was not lost however, as President Monroe took the opportunity to appoint him as the country's first Ambassador to Russia.

John Quincy Adams, Abigail's son and the 6th President, recalled that he used to watch his mother melt pewter and make bullets for the war effort with this mold.

Using His International Skills

In 1812, he was part of a delegation to Belgium that negotiated a peace treaty to end the War of 1812 between the U.S. and Great Britain. And from 1817 to 1825, he served as Secretary of State under President James Monroe. He was so successful in that role that he set up procedures for the State Department that remained in place for decades.

Failing, at First, and Trying Again

He was elected president by a slim majority. But the losing candidate was so bitter, he organized a resistance movement in Congress that successfully blocked every proposal that President John Quincy Adams made. He did not win re-election.

Yet, he did not sulk away. He was elected to the U.S. Congress and represented Massachusetts for nine consecutive terms. He was known as "Old Man Eloquent" for his speech-making, as everytime he stood to speak, the room hushed, and all the Senators turned to listen. Moreover, he was one of the leaders of the abolition movement in the Senate, the movement to free the enslaved population. In 1841, he successfully argued before the Supreme Court for the freedom of the enslaved Africans who had mutinied aboard the Spanish slave ship, Amistad.*

The Presidential Footprint

Most historians agree that President John Quincy Adams' tenure as president was a failure. While President John Quincy Adams did not leave a legacy from his presidency, his work as Senator, Congressman, and Secretary of State had a profound effect on the country. As Secretary of State, he established the U.S./Canadian border, and negotiated treaties that gave Americans two generations of peace with European countries. As a lawyer and Senator, he argued landmark cases before the Supreme Court and opened the Senate for debate on slavery.

*For comprehension and vocabulary work, see the *Discussion Guide*, page 15.

Birth: July 11, 1767 **Place:** Braintree, Massachusetts **Occupation:** Lawyer, Senator, Diplomat

Religion: Unitarian **Term of Office:** 1825 to 1829 **Death:** February 23, 1848

Position on Slavery: Objected to the Missouri Compromise. Called it a proslavery conspiracy.

- As an ambassador, he added language to a treaty that would have banned the international slave trade.
- As a Congressman, he spent eight years laboring to dissolve a "gag rule" in Congress that immediately "tabled without debate any petition critical of slavery."
- He regularly demanded that the hundreds of anti-slavery petitions he received be read into the daily Congressional Record.
- The "gag rule" was finally dissolved in 1844 due to his efforts.

Andrew Jackson

Becoming a Frontiersman

Andrew Jackson was the thorn in President John Quincy Adams' side, blocking every effort he made during Adams' term. When President Jackson was elected, he represented a new era, the competition between the self-made man and the traditionally educated man. He was the first president to break the mold of the Virginia and New England aristocracies.

Jackson was born in a log cabin, somewhere along the border of North and South Carolina, on the frontier where death was widespread. His father died before he was born, so his mother moved in with her sister's family. When the Revolutionary War broke out, he and his brothers fought with the "irregulars," being too young for formal enlistment. Although the obvious dangers were from battles, his brothers and mother all died from disease. By his fifteenth birthday, the war was over, and he was orphaned.

7th President of the United States

Owning the Self-Made Man

With no place to go, the youth wandered and eventually settled down in North Carolina to study law. In 1788, he moved to Nashville to build his law practice. Cases were few, so he also dabbled in the trading business and was slowly able to buy land. With it, he married and embraced the Southern lifestyle of slave owner.

His law practice kept him in touch with the community, who elected him to his first office in 1795. He was a delegate to the state constitutional convention. Then he served as Tennessee's first congressman, then senator, and eventually governor of the Tennessee territory. Reclaiming his law practice, he came home to sit on Tennessee's superior court.

Major General Andrew Jackson

His youthful attraction to the soldier's life returned to him in midlife, so he joined the Tennessee militia to fight against an Indian faction of Creeks. Jackson fought alongside European and Indian allies, and together they overcame the Creek offensive in 1814. In May of 1814, he was made major general of the entire southern frontier and spent the next several years negotiating Indian treaties. In January 1815, he became a hero after he led the charge and stopped the British attack on New Orleans, becoming as admired as George Washington. In 1824, he resigned from the army and returned to Tennessee.

President Andrew Jackson

In 1828, he was elected President of the United States. By that time, Jackson had served over ten years in the army and fought the British, Spanish, and the native Indians. He had also served with native Indian allies. Accordingly, his gruff frontier manner projected a distinct national character that became known as the Age of Jacksonian Democracy. It was an era in which the government began to treat Indian culture as inferior. Although he did not dislike Indians, Jackson thought the American culture was superior.

Yet, the Cherokee had developed a written language, which they spread through its use in a newspaper. They had also written self-government documents claiming their sovereignty over their own lands. Although the U.S. Supreme Court agreed with them, the state of Georgia rejected the national judicial authority over the states' territories.

President Jackson agreed with Georgia and worked to pass The Indian Removal Act in Congress. Although it was a complicated process to force the Indians to move, President Jackson worked personally to bring it about. The forced migration was later called "The Trail of Tears" because of the death, disease, and hardship inflicted on the tribes.*

The Presidential Footprint

As President Jackson was a strong politician who carved a new path quite different in tone from previous presidents, he was accused of bringing the monarchy back to America. His political opponents nicknamed him "King Andrew" and formed the Whig party—a reference to their objection to the formal wigs worn by British Lords. They objected to President Jackson's domineering decision-making. Thus, President Jackson's greatest legacy was the birth of the two-party political system, which remains to this day.

*For comprehension and vocabulary work, see the *Discussion Guide*, page 16.

Birth: March 15, 1767   **Place:** Waxhaw, South Carolina   **Occupation:** Lawyer, Soldier

Religion: Presbyterian   **Term of Office:** 1829 to 1837   **Death:** June 8, 1845

Position on Slavery: He enslaved ninety-five persons on his Tennessee plantation.

- President Jackson used enslaved labor to build the North Portico on the White House.
- He brought enslaved individuals to the White House from his home and purchased more to run the White House during his presidency.

Martin Van Buren

Claiming American Citizenship

Martin Van Buren was one of six children and the first president who had not been born as a British citizen. He was born at the end of the Revolutionary War in a Dutch settlement in upstate New York.

8th President of the United States

The Van Burens were not wealthy. In addition to being a farmer and innkeeper, Martin's father held a part-time job as town clerk and rented out the inn for political meetings. Martin attended a one-room schoolhouse until he was fourteen, and never went to college, which was not the custom for most young men of Martin's class. However, the fact that he went to school until age 14 was unusual for a family who needed their children to bring in income.

Taking Advantage of Social Ties

As an innkeeper and town clerk, Martin's dad had many social connections. Utilizing his inn as a political meeting place brought many people in government to his establishment. Activating these acquaintances, he secured Martin an apprenticeship with a lawyer. By age 17, Martin was reading law at night and working as a law clerk during the day.

In 1803, at 21 years of age, he opened a law practice in Kinderhook, earning a reputation, and a large income, arguing land claims for the working classes against landowners who had old colonial British claims. Thus, his successes contributed to the emerging new quality of American culture that favored the common man.

Maneuvering Through New York Politics

To be sure, politics in New York were changing, and Martin sought connections with the newer generation. Although the older generation liked him, he deftly deflected their attention while nurturing relationships with the younger politicians. In behaving this way, many people thought he was untrustworthy because he kept his own political views secret. Nevertheless, he moved up the New York political ladder until he was elected Senator in the United States Congress in 1821.

As Senator, he backed the Jeffersonian concept of states' supremacy over a strong federal government. Consequently, he supported Andrew Jackson for president since he had become the heir to that viewpoint. With Jackson, Martin Van Buren took the side of the self-made man who was becoming the heart of American culture.

In 1828, Jackson appointed Van Buren Secretary of State. In that position, he ended up in fierce opposition to Jackson's Vice President, John Calhoun, who stood for a

Photo Credit: National Portrait Gallery, Smithsonian Institution; gift of Mrs. Robert Timpson Conserved with funds from the Smithsonian Women's Committee

view of state's rights so extreme that the two became angry rivals. In fact, Van Buren had helped President Jackson formulate his response to these extremists by saying, "The Union: it must be preserved."

Taking the Oath of Presidential Office

In his inauguration speech, Van Buren pledged to faithfully follow in the popular President Jackson's footsteps. However, in his first national crisis, Van Buren dropped Jackson's policies.

The country was in a dire financial tailspin called the Panic of 1837. President Van Buren proposed an independent national banking system, which would oversee the state-level banks. It was a solution in line with a strong federal government, and Congress hotly debated it.

Even with Van Buren's experience navigating the murky political waters in New York State, he was unable to convince Congress to approve it. Finally in 1840, Congress passed the national banking bill, but the country had suffered for three years—many Americans in near starvation—before Van Buren succeeded.*

The Presidential Footprint

Although President Van Buren was criticized for abandoning Jackson's economic views, he was also criticized when he followed Jackson's other policies. Van Buren fulfilled the Indian removal project, the Trail of Tears, with what many thought was a heartless and cruel vigor. With both issues on voters' minds, he was not re-elected. Historians credit Van Buren with a strong contribution to the development of the Democratic party, while recognizing that his strong state-level negotiating skills left him a weak negotiator on the national scene.

*For comprehension and vocabulary work, as well as a mini-lesson on The Bank War, see the *Discussion Guide*, pages 17-18.

Birth: December 5, 1782   **Place:** Kinderhook, New York   **Occupation:** Lawyer

Religion: Dutch Reformed   **Term of Office:** 1837 to 1841   **Death:** July 24, 1862

Position on Slavery: His father owned six enslaved persons.

- When Martin was 17 and studying law, New York passed a gradual emancipation law, which freed those born into slavery at certain milestones.

- During Martin's New York political career, New York Congress passed a law that required freed black men to own property worth $250 to vote.

- During his presidency, his staff included 5 freed and 4 enslaved persons working in the White House.

William Henry Harrison

Inheriting a Proud History

William Harrison was born into a politically famous, slave-owning family in Virginia. His father, Benjamin had served as governor and signed the Declaration of Independence. His parents were also close friends with George and Martha Washington.

Tutors came to his home to teach young William until college. In that era, land passed to the eldest son, and since William was the youngest, he had no hope for wealth. His father helped him by apprenticing him to a well-known physician. But William was not interested in medicine. When his father died in 1791, William was free, and he chose a military career.

9th President of the United States

Seeking Fame

During this period, war was raging throughout North America. Even though the Revolutionary War just ended, the British continued to fight in the West and along the Canadian border. The French also defended their territory, while the Native peoples allied with whatever nation would help them preserve their lands.

For a young man looking for fame and fortune, the soldier's life offered possibilities. William Harrison enlisted as an Ensign, the lowest officer's rank, but soon rose to Lieutenant. Stationed at Fort Washington, near Cincinnati, he fought to protect settlers. Because British agents encouraged Indians to attack, there were plenty of chances for William to gain fame. Soon he was promoted to Captain, took command of Fort Washington, and married.

Using Family Connections

His father-in-law was a judge in the territory and didn't like him. Angry that his son-in-law was poor, he used his connection with President John Adams to get Harrison appointed secretary of the Northwest Territory, the land that eventually became Michigan, Ohio, Indiana, Illinois, Minnesota, and Wisconsin.

In that role, he gained settlers' approval by changing land-buying policies to allow smaller purchases, paid for with four-year payment plans. He eventually became governor of the territories, with orders from Presidents Adams and Jefferson to claim as much land from the Indians as possible.

Returning to the Military

Governor Harrison forced legal treaties that took advantage of Native Americans. In one, he manipulated the terms to illegally take about 51 million acres. When he initiated a similar deal with tribes who were not recognized as owners of the land in previous treaties, Chief Tecumseh became angry. He organized several tribes, with British allies, to fight the Americans.

Governor Harrison got permission to command the troops, even though he had retired thirteen years previously. After a few victories, he was promoted to Brigadier General, while Chief Tecumseh was killed leading his men in the fierce fighting. Although General Harrison's negotiations for land were not ethical, his battle victories earned him fame.

Attending Parties and Campaigning for Office

With the war still raging, Harrison resigned from the military and went on a public relations tour. He was celebrated everywhere and soaked up the attention with a remarkable lack of humility, then returned to his civilian life. He was only forty-one and spent the next twenty-five years running campaigns for political offices, most of which he did not win.

He spent one term in the U.S. House of Representatives, one term as a Representative in the Ohio legislature, and one term as a U. S. Senator.

President William Henry Harrison

In the election of 1840, the country was attracted to William Harrison as a war hero and a member of the Virginia aristocracy. He won and wrote a two-hour long inauguration speech. The day was rainy, and President Harrison did not wear a coat. He became ill with pneumonia and died one month later.*

The Presidential Footprint

President William Harrison spent almost no time in the presidency. So his legacy is largely assessed based on his work as Governor of the Northwest Territories. Although he was popular among the settlers, he was instrumental in the demise of the Native Americans.

*For comprehension and vocabulary work, see the *Discussion Guide*, page 19.

Birth: February 9, 1773 **Place:** Charles City County, Virginia **Occupation:** Soldier

Religion: Episcopalian **Term of Office:** 1841 **Death:** April 4, 1841

Position on Slavery and Native Americans: William was born into Virginia's aristocratic plantation families.

- He believed that the fate of slavery should be left up to individual states.
- He earned a reputation as an unrelenting fighter against Native Americans.
- He signed many treaties that gave European settlers millions of acres, and the native Indians only pennies.

John Tyler

Deciding on a Career Path

John Tyler received the best education of the day. At seventeen, he graduated from college and began studying law under his father. At 19 in 1809, he was a practicing lawyer. John benefited from his father's connections as a former Governor of Virginia and was hired by the law firm of the first Attorney General of the United States.

Yet even with an ideal job, he decided to move into politics. He was appointed to the Virginia House of Delegates just when the movement began against the establishment of a National Bank. He agreed with other Southerners who saw it as a tool for a powerful central government to interfere with states' rights.

10th President of the United States

Going to War Almost, and Coming Home

When the War of 1812 started, while Presidents Jackson and Harrison both fought and made names for themselves, Tyler enlisted and trained, but never saw combat. He was quickly back in Washington taking up the fight against the establishment of a powerful central government.

He also argued against the Missouri Compromise of 1820. He thought the federal government should not have any control over whether slavery would be allowed in a state, supporting the right of individual states to decide for themselves. As the anti-slavery faction succeeded, Tyler resigned from Congress in 1821.

After a few years, he was appointed Senator from Virginia and continued the fight against a national treasury system. In 1840, John Tyler was selected to be Vice President with candidate William Harrison. During the inauguration, Tyler left the city and went home to his farm in the Virginia countryside. One month later, a messenger arrived at dawn with a message that President Harrison had died.

Sweeping Away the Emergency

Vice President Tyler rushed to Washington and found President Harrison's cabinet in distress. They were not sure what to do, since no President had ever died in office. Was John Tyler to be a temporary president? Should they hold new elections?

Tyler resolved the issue by sweeping it away with the confident explanation that the Constitution supported his claim to the presidency. He immediately took the oath of office and promised the country he would implement President Harrison's policies.

Setting a Precedent

Although President Tyler did a great service to the country by setting a precedent for this situation, his presidency was weak from then on. He was never able to compromise with the cabinet. None of the cabinet members would support him. In very short order, he had no friends in Congress either, which worked quickly to revise a law to establish a National Bank. When it came to President Tyler's desk to sign, he vetoed it.

A second bill, with further revisions came to his desk, and he vetoed that one too. Nearly his entire cabinet resigned in protest. During the first two years of his presidency, many new Cabinet appointees were named, and most quickly quit. Congress tried to impeach President Tyler, but that effort also failed. However, on his last day in office, Congress succeeded in overriding his veto of a law to provide funding for some new ships.*

The Presidential Footprint

Although President Tyler was not a successful president, his quick action to take the oath of office set an example for a peaceful transfer of power in the case of a president's death. In every case since then, vice presidents have stepped into the office when the president died. Also, it was the first time that Congress used their powers to impeach a president, and the first time Congress overrode a presidential veto. These two Congressional actions were important tests that proved the systems of checks and balances worked.

*For comprehension and vocabulary work, see the *Discussion Guide*, page 20.

Birth: March 29, 1790   **Place:** Charles City County, Virginia   **Occupation:** Lawyer

Religion: Episcopalian   **Term of Office:** 1841 to 1845   **Death:** January 18, 1862

Position on Slavery: John Tyler was born into a Virginia aristocratic plantation family and kept about forty-six enslaved persons.

- He did not allow overseers to whip enslaved persons and refused to allow families to be split up.
- President Tyler had two enslaved persons serve as servants in the White House.
- President Tyler also hired a "colored man" named Wilkins to be head butler at the White House, the first Black American to hold that position.
- In 1864, Union troops entered President Tyler's property and freed his slaves.

James K. Polk

Growing Up in North Carolina

James Knox Polk was the eldest in a strictly religious family. He had nine brothers and sisters, all raised on a plantation run by enslaved labor. James' mother and paid tutors taught him to read and write at home until 1816, when he registered at the University of North Carolina.

He graduated two years later, then studied law under a well-known lawyer in Nashville, who became Attorney General under President Martin Van Buren. With these connections, James got a job as a clerk for the Tennessee Senate, handling all the paperwork that senators produced, such as proposals for laws. He became a lawyer in 1820.

11th President of the United States

Finding a Mentor

By 1823, he was working for the Tennessee House of Representatives as assistant to the Governor. He had a reputation for working hard, earning him respect and seven terms as a United States Representative in Washington. Moreover, he was a strong supporter of Tennessee's favorite son, President Andrew Jackson. The two formed a close bond that lasted throughout James' career.

In 1839, James left Washington to take the Governorship of Tennessee, following in his mentor's footsteps. James and President Jackson worked so closely together, that during the economic depression of the late 1830s, many people blamed them both for the bank failures and farm foreclosures. Governor Polk took the brunt of the blame and lost his bid for re-election in 1841. He went back to his plantation and bided his time.

In 1844, he got his chance to run for President. Sectionalism was gaining strength, that is, voters were putting the needs of their region ahead of the needs of the country. And the two biggest issues were the expansion of slavery into new territories, and Texas' bid to join the union. Polk won the election by the slimmest margin in U.S. history, taking the oath of office on March 4, 1845.

President James K. Polk

With Polk's extensive experience in government, it may have been natural that he saw the need for an independent national treasury system. After decades of debate, President Polk finally signed it into law.

Yet, whether to allow slavery in new territories was the most controversial issue facing the nation during President Polk's term. The issue was tangled up with Manifest Destiny, the belief that God had ordained Americans to take over the land and spread their ideals. Whether that included slavery was hotly debated.

The issue surged when Congress approved Texas' application, whereupon President Polk sent an ambassador to Mexico with instructions to buy California and settle other border issues. The Mexican military angrily took up arms, vowing to recover all the lost Mexican land, starting with a raid into Texas that killed eleven Americans. The Mexican-American War had begun.

Protesting the War and Drawing the Line

One lone contrarian and first-term representative from Illinois, named Abe Lincoln, was among the very few who voted against the war. Mr. Lincoln decisively denounced the claim that American blood had been shed, insisting that it was a contrived reason for war.

Nonetheless, the United States won the war. As a result, they settled on the Rio Grande as the border and purchased California and New Mexico from the Mexican government. President Polk favored extending the line separating the North from the South, as set up in the Missouri Compromise. That meant that slavery would extend all the way across the South, including into Southern California.*

By 1849 as his only term as President was over, sectionalism was stronger than ever, with slavery as its number one issue.

During President Polk's term, Dred and Harriet Scott sued their white enslaver on April 6, 1846 in the St. Louis Courthouse. Since he had brought them into free states, where they had lived for extended periods, they sued for their freedom.

The Presidential Footprint

Although President Polk finalized the American borders, he did so at the cost of sectional differences that remained unresolved. Some historians have criticized him for not recognizing the depth of sensitivity in the country over the issue of slavery. By ignoring it, feelings began festering and were set to explode in twelve years' time.

*For comprehension and vocabulary work, see the *Discussion Guide*, page 21.

Birth: November 2, 1795 **Place:** Mecklenburg County, North Carolina **Occupation:** Lawyer

Religion: Presbyterian **Term of Office:** 1845 to 1849 **Death:** June 15, 1849

Position on Slavery: James K. Polk owned a plantation in Tennessee, supported by enslaved labor.

- President Polk regularly separated enslaved families and purchased at least thirteen children separately from their parents.
- He had many problems with runaway slaves, which he solved by buying land and moving enslaved persons further south into Mississippi.
- During his White House years, he secretly purchased nineteen enslaved people.
- Since he died first, his will requested that his wife free all the slaves upon her death.

Zachary Taylor

Growing Up on the Kentucky Frontier

Zachary Taylor was one of seven children who lived in a small cabin on the Kentucky frontier. As his father prospered, dependent upon enslaved laborers, he added on to their house until it was a comfortable brick home. His father ambitiously pushed his ownership to 10,000 acres and twenty-six enslaved individuals.

Young Zachary received a fine education but was never a scholar. From his earliest boyhood, he had set his sights on the military. By 1808, he was commanding the troops at Fort Pickering near Memphis.

12th President of the United States

Respecting Indians and Defending Settlers

Most of his duties were to defend American settlers from Indians, and that kept him moving from fort to fort throughout the West. Despite his official duties, he found that he respected the Indians' fighting abilities and dedication to their people. Often, he worried about his own troops who were frequently poorly trained. He believed that the best course of action was to place his troops between the settlers and the Indian tribes to separate them, and that fighting between the two groups was pointless.

He gained fame with victories in the Mexican-American War, during which he was known to fight alongside his troops, even in hand-to-hand combat. He delivered victories routinely and in swift succession against armies much larger than his own. The American newspapers were ecstatic, heaping praise on General Zachary Taylor and comparing him to George Washington and Andrew Jackson.

Accepting the Presidency

During his entire career, President Taylor had been silent about his politics, had never joined a political party, nor had he ever voted. After his victories in the war, many called for his candidacy. Southerners assumed that he supported the right of individual states to determine their own position on slavery.

On the contrary, he believed that it made no sense to expand slavery into western areas because neither cotton nor sugar could grow in those climates.

Also contrary to what other Southerners believed, he thought the country needed a strong banking system. Whereas many Southerners feared that a strong national bank would threaten their plantation economies.

So, in response to calls for him to run for President, he decided to join the Whig party. Southerners were dismayed. Many others did not think he was qualified to be President. Some voters recognized that he did not have any real understanding of political systems. Nevertheless, he won with 163 electoral college votes to his opponent's 127.

President Taylor believed that he should only veto legislation that was unconstitutional. Thus, he did not engage with Congress in the legislative process, nor make any attempts to resolve disputes. He let Congress develop laws to govern the country without interference.

One bill making its way through Congress was the so-called Compromise of 1850. The bill, if passed, would allow California to enter the union as a free state, and the Mexico territories to decide by popular, local vote whether to allow slavery. It also included a fugitive slave law which would require northerners to return runaways to their southern enslavers. This effectively declared the federal government as protectors of the "peculiar institution" of slavery, a position which northern abolitionists could not abide.

President Taylor opposed the compromise, but his threat to veto it ultimately didn't matter. He only served for about sixteen months. Then in July of 1850, he became ill with what doctors called "cholera morbus." He suffered from severe stomach pains and died five days later.*

The Presidential Footprint

His only impactful act was to steer the Clayton-Bulwer Treaty to ratification. It was a treaty with England stating that each country would not attempt any control over any canal that might be built across Nicaragua. In effect, the treaty weakened the U.S.'s commitment to Manifest Destiny. Yet it opened an era of interest in Central America that became a guiding factor throughout the rest of the nineteenth century.

*For comprehension and vocabulary work, see the *Discussion Guide*, page 23.

Birth: November 24, 1784   **Place:** Barboursville, Virginia   **Occupation:** Soldier

Religion: Episcopalian   **Term of Office:** 1849 to 1850   **Death:** July 9, 1850

Position on Slavery: Zachary Taylor owned thousands of acres in Mississippi and Louisiana, all supported with enslaved persons.

- He purchased eighty-one enslaved persons, including children.
- Historians believe he was the last President with enslaved persons in the White House.
- He purchased a plantation and sixty-four enslaved persons for his son.

Millard Fillmore

Pulling Himself Out of Poverty

Millard Fillmore was the second child of eight children. Living on a farm with poor, rocky soil, his parents struggled to feed their children. Millard's father, as poor families of this era often did, arranged for Millard to be apprenticed to a cloth maker. It was one less mouth to feed, and Millard would learn a trade.

While Millard lived with the cloth maker, he secretly bought a dictionary and used it to try learning new words. He could barely read, yet he was eager to learn. He longed to escape from his master's cruelty, not an unusual situation for many of these apprenticeship arrangements. Millard hated his circumstances and cloth making. As soon as he was able, he borrowed money to buy out his contract and walked back home, about 100 miles away.

13th President of the United States

Getting an Education

Millard was determined to get an education, and so he walked to the schoolhouse in a nearby town. The teacher was only two years older than him, but he accepted her encouragment to read. He was a voracious learner, and she was the first person in his life to support his goals. His father saw his dedication and realized that he might, after all, have the stamina to become a lawyer. To his father's credit, he sought out a local judge who agreed to accept Millard as a private law student.

Young Millard passed the bar in 1823 and set up a law practice near Albany, New York. Soon, he was active in state politics. He served three terms in the state legislature and actively began pushing through laws that ended the practice of imprisoning debtors. These laws made Representative Fillmore popular throughout the state, and he was handily elected to the U.S. House of Representatives in 1832.

In 1848, he won the Vice President spot on Candidate Zachary Taylor's presidential ticket. As was common in those days, they did not campaign together, so neither man really knew the other. When they met in Washington, the President took an immediate dislike to Vice President Fillmore. As a result, they did not work together, and Fillmore knew nothing of President Taylor's administration, work style, or opinions. In sixteen months, after the President's sudden death, Millard Fillmore took the oath of office and became President.

Facing Resistance

On his first day in office, President Taylor's cabinet, who were southern supporters, all resigned. Issues surrounding slavery consumed the political scene. Heated debates over new territories' rights and numerous failed compromises had kept Congress stalled for years.

In particular, President Fillmore knew that his views on the Compromise of 1850 bill were different from Taylor's who had planned to veto the bill. Whereas Fillmore had told Taylor during his illness that he planned to use his vice-presidential vote to break the tie in the Senate and pass the bill.

The bill would have allowed California to become a state without slavery and the Fugitive Slave Act to pass. It also required all persons who escaped from slavery, when found, to be sent back to the South. Basically, it forced Northern abolitionists to support slavery. President Fillmore believed that compromise was the only way to hold the Union together. He was disappointed that the bill failed to pass.

In 1850, while Dred Scott was appealing his case, Congress passed the Fugitive Slave Bill. It required Northerners to return any runaway to his enslaver in the South.

Instead, Congress divided the issues and fought through five smaller bills, passing all of them, including the Fugitive Slave Act. President Fillmore signed them all.*

The Presidential Footprint

The Compromise of 1850 gave most Americans a little something to be happy about. Yet, most Americans found much more to dislike in it. Tensions within the country increased after its passage, as the United States found itself inching ever closer to a civil war.

*For comprehension and vocabulary work, see the *Discussion Guide*, page 23.

Birth: January 7, 1800   **Place:** Summerhill, New York   **Occupation:** Lawyer

Religion: Unitarian   **Term of Office:** 1850 to 1853   **Death:** March 8, 1874

Position on Slavery: Millard Fillmore was born into extreme poverty on a farm in upstate New York. The family owned no enslaved persons.

- President Fillmore supported the Compromise of 1850, which required Northern non-slave states to capture and return anyone who had escaped slavery.

Franklin Pierce

Inheriting a Prestigious History

The earliest Pierces settled in New Hampshire as Puritans in the 1620s. During the Revolutionary War, Benjamin Pierce fought and led his troops to several victories. Thus, he enjoyed great respect and honor among the citizens of the area. When young Franklin was born, he benefited from his father's reputation, attending local public schools and then private college.

At college, making friends was a priority for Franklin, and his grades suffered. For a while he was failing, until he decided to apply himself, ultimately graduating fifth from the top of his class. His social skills included a natural speaking ability, which supported his courtroom work as a lawyer.

14th President of the United States

Falling In with the Family Business

He was handsome, well-spoken, well-connected, and was elected to the state House of Representatives in 1829. By 1831 he was Speaker of the House, the leader of the House of Representatives, while his father was Governor. Both father and son were strong supporters of President Andrew Jackson, and when Franklin Pierce was elected to the U.S. House of Representatives, he supported Jacksonian policies.

Falling Back on Old Habits

In 1837, Franklin Pierce became the U.S. Senator from New Hampshire. Although he was popular in Washington, he wrote no laws and gained a reputation as a partier. The only cause that he had any genuine interest in was to work against the abolitionists, or those who wanted to abolish slavery. His friends in the Washington crowd were mostly Southerners, and he had come to sympathize with their cause.

His wife, who was opposed to all drinking, may also have had some influence over him because in 1841, Franklin resigned from the Senate and returned home to his law practice. He quit drinking and became so skilled in argument before the court, that people from around the state came to the courtroom to hear him speak.

Aspiring to National Office

He enjoyed the fame he earned. With his eye still on a political career, he had seen how his father's military service garnered him honor and respect. So, Franklin enlisted in the military as a low-ranking private in the army. Eager for quick accolades, he reached out to President James Polk for a commission. Franklin was well known in Washington circles, so by 1847, he was Brigadier General Franklin Pierce, without any military experience. It showed. During a battle in Mexico, he fell off his horse, incurred a severe leg injury, and passed out from the pain. The soldiers called him "Fainting Frank."

Favoring the Local Vote

In 1852, he won the Presidency, not because he was popular in New Hampshire, but because nationally, he was less well known. Most voters had no reason to dislike him. Nevertheless, there was no way to hide from the white-hot debate in the country over slavery in the new states.

The latest to the controversy were Kansas and Nebraska. So-called "free-soilers" were abolitionists who wanted the states to enter the Union without slavery. Others who proposed "popular sovereignty" wanted the voters within each state to decide whether to allow slavery. This group supported slavery.

The Missouri Compromise of 1820 had banned slavery in Kansas and Nebraska because they were north of a pre-designated latitude. One Illinois Senator with Southern colleagues in Congress was proposing a new law that would wipe out the old Missouri Compromise. It was called the Kansas-Nebraska Act, and it allowed the territories to decide for themselves, in a local vote, whether to allow slavery.

President Pierce signed it. In very short order, Kansas became a bellwether of what was to come. Fighting broke out in Kansas, earning it the nickname "Bleeding Kansas."*

The Presidential Footprint

Although President Franklin Pierce was not highly qualified to be President, some historians point out that none of the Presidents between Jackson and Lincoln served more than one term. The scorching debates over slavery, increasing with each decade, demanded strong leadership. Neither President Franklin Pierce's friendliness nor his party loyalty was strong enough to withstand the coming events.

*For comprehension and vocabulary work, see the *Discussion Guide*, page 24.

Birth: November 23, 1804   **Place:** Hillsborough, New Hampshire   **Occupation:** Lawyer, Public Official

Religion: Episcopalian   **Term of Office:** 1853 to 1857   **Death:** October 8, 1869

Position on Slavery: Franklin Pierce was a Northerner who fully supported the institution of slavery.

- He supported the Compromise of 1850, including the Fugitive Slave Act, which required Northerners to return escapees to the South.

- He supported the Kansas-Nebraska Act, which led to bloodshed in Kansas and was the final powder keg leading to the Civil War.

James Buchanan

Watching the Westward Migration

James Buchanan was the second of eleven children born to Irish immigrants who lived in a log cabin in Pennsylvania, located in a mountain pass that settlers had to travel through on their way West. James Buchanan, Sr. operated barns, stables, an orchard, and a store on this last stop for many miles and outfitted all settlers passing through.

James was an able student and entered college when he was sixteen. He was a somewhat rowdy youth and was nearly expelled from college twice. But he managed to wipe his slate clean and graduate with honors in only two years. In 1813 at 22, he passed the bar and began practicing law in Lancaster, Pennsylvania. He proved to be a gifted orator and lawyer, but the War of 1812 interrupted, and he enlisted. His regiment was never sent to the front, and he soon returned home.

15th President of the United States

Serving in Congress

His legal practice grew, and he became a very wealthy and respected lawyer, serving in Congress from 1821 through 1831. In 1832, President Andrew Jackson appointed him to be the U.S. Ambassador to Russia. One of his greatest accomplishments was finalizing a treaty with Russia that had been in discussion for many years.

When he came home, he was elected to the U.S. Senate just as the slavery issue was flaring up. Although there is some evidence that he personally disliked the practice, he nevertheless defended it. He believed the Constitution provided for individual states to determine their own destiny and that abolitionists were unpatriotic. Many times, he stated that they were self-righteous in denying Southerners the right to their own way of life.

He became one of the most powerful Senators in Congress and hoped to gain the Presidency, but it eluded him four times. Later, President James Polk appointed him the Ambassadorship to England. The job kept him out of the fray over slavery back home. When he returned, he did not have a sullied reputation.

Interfering with the Supreme Court

James Buchanan was elected President in 1856 and took the oath of office the following Spring. Throughout the tensions over slavery, lawyer Buchanan had held great faith in the judicial system. He had often urged the public to let the Supreme Court decide the issue. Then two days before his inauguration, he secretly urged a Northern judge on the court to side with Southern judges in the Dred Scott case.

The country had been anxiously awaiting this verdict. Dred Scott was a man enslaved by an army doctor who served at various army posts in states that outlawed slavery. Scott argued in court that he was therefore entitled to his freedom. The tension in the country was electrifying, so in President Buchanan's inaugural address, he pleaded for calm, assuring his listeners that the Supreme Court would be issuing a ruling to settle the matter once and for all.

Two days later, the Supreme Court announced its decision: that enslaved persons were not citizens and therefore could not bring cases against their masters; that enslaved persons had no right to trial by jury. In fact, the ruling also declared that the Missouri Compromise, in which slavery was outlawed in many new territories, was unconstitutional. Abolitionists exploded in anger. Southerners took it as vindication.

President Buchanan tried to calm the public by appointing people from both sides to his cabinet. Yet the situation in "Bleeding Kansas" increased the tensions further. Back and forth, the residents in the Kansas territory wrote different state constitutions that alternately allowed and disallowed slavery. When Kansas finally entered the union as a free state, violent outbursts exploded around the state. The President did nothing because he believed they should work it out themselves.*

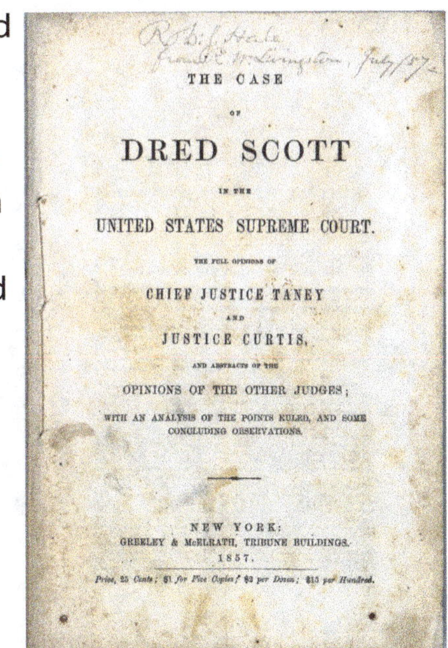

In 1857, the Supreme Court ruled that Americans of African descent could not be citizens of the United States, because historically "they had no rights that the white man was bound to respect."

The Presidential Footprint

Because Buchanan tried to stay neutral in the fight over slavery, many historians say that he did nothing to calm the nation. His neutrality led straight to the Civil War.

*For comprehension and vocabulary work, see the *Discussion Guide*, page 25.

Birth: April 23, 1791 **Place:** Cove Gap, Pennsylvania **Occupation:** Lawyer

Religion: Presbyterian **Term of Office:** 1857 to 1861 **Death:** June 1, 1868

Position on Slavery: James Buchanan's father bought and sold Black indentured servants, under Pennsylvania's Gradual Abolition Act of 1780, which created stages of servitude and freedom.

- After his father died, James Buchanan managed the sale of two Black indentured servants, one of whom had "about six years to serve." Some historians use the phrase "term slavery" to describe Black Americans' conditions in states like Pennsylvania.

- For Buchanan, the Constitution provided for slavery, and as a lawyer, he worked diligently to uphold that law.

Dred Scott and the Supreme Court

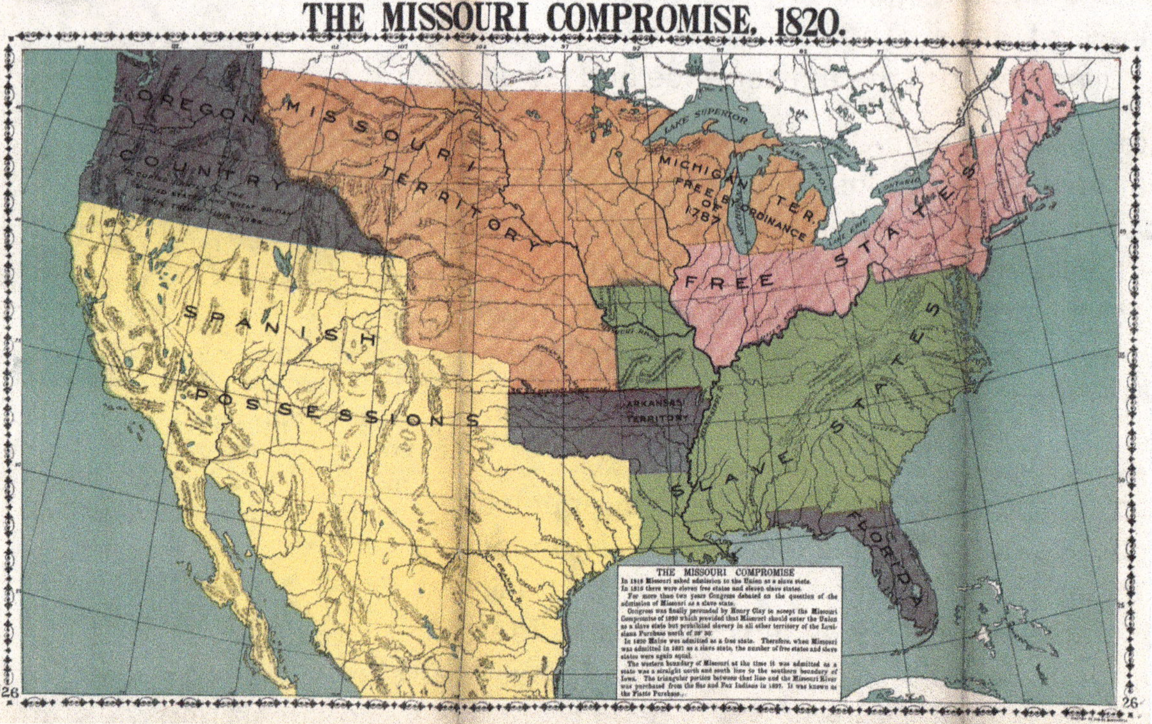

Missouri was admitted as a slave state, even though it lies north of the accepted border between North and South.

Dred and Harriet Scott sued for their freedom on April 6, 1846 in the St. Louis Courthouse. Since their white enslaver had brought them into free states, where they had lived for extended periods, they sued for their freedom.

R. S. J. Hale
from E. W. Livingston, July/57
THE CASE
OF
DRED SCOTT
IN THE
UNITED STATES SUPREME COURT.
THE FULL OPINIONS OF
CHIEF JUSTICE TANEY
AND
JUSTICE CURTIS,
AND ABSTRACTS OF THE
OPINIONS OF THE OTHER JUDGES;
WITH AN ANALYSIS OF THE POINTS RULED, AND SOME CONCLUDING OBSERVATIONS.

NEW YORK:
GREELEY & McELRATH, TRIBUNE BUILDINGS.
1857.
Price, 25 Cents; $1 for Five Copies; $2 per Dozen; $15 per Hundred.

In 1857, the Supreme Court ruled that Americans of African descent could not be citizens of the United States, because historically "they had no rights that the white man was bound to respect."

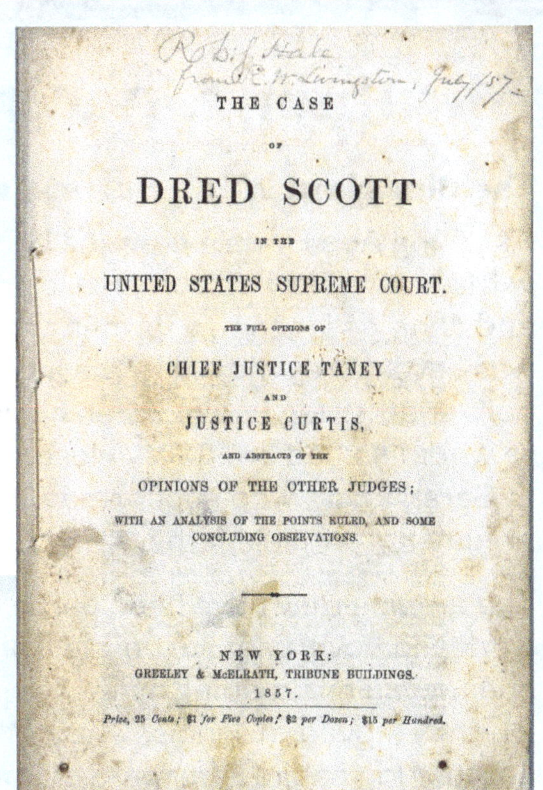

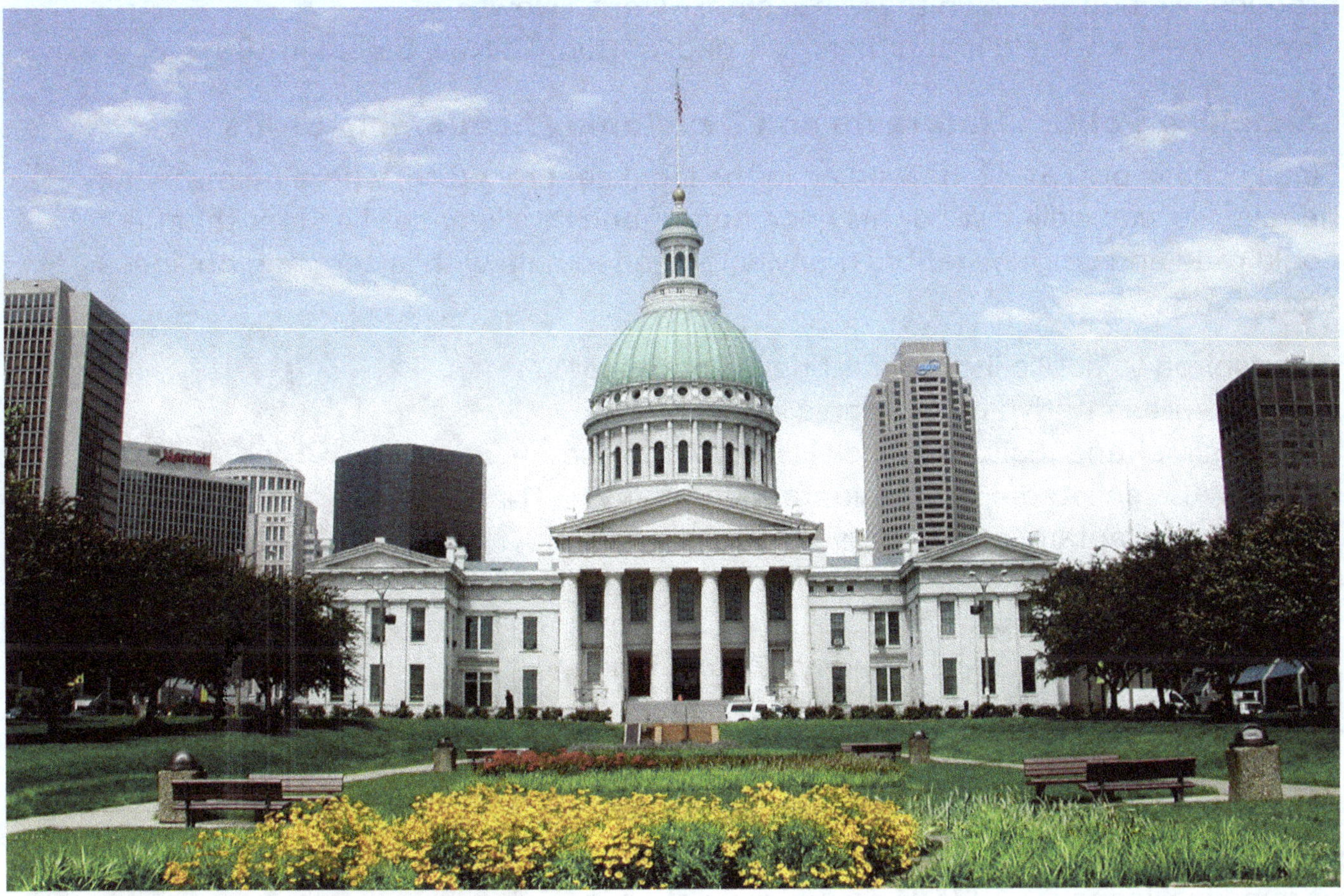

Dred Scott first brought his lawsuit to this courthouse in St. Louis.

Abraham Lincoln

Tackling Hard Work, Sorrow, and Self-Reliance

As young Abe Lincoln grew, he became well-acquainted with sorrow. He was born in a log cabin to Nancy Hanks and Thomas Lincoln, a farmer and carpenter. When Abe was seven, they moved to the Indiana wilderness and built another log cabin. When he was 9, his mother died, to whom he had been very close. His dad married again to Sarah Bush, who supported Abe during his frequent arguments with his father.

The arguing may have been partly caused by the hard work and poverty of life on the frontier. For rest, Abe spent evenings reading by the fireplace. When he was 21, they moved to Illinois, where Abe helped build yet another log cabin. Afterward, he tried to leave home, building a flatboat and filling it with customers' farm produce. He floated down the Mississippi River to New Orleans where he sold it and then returned, settling in New Salem in 1831.

16th President of the United States

Launching Political Interests and Developing Leadership Skills

Finally on his own at 22, he worked in the local general store, where he met many people. He was well-liked for his good humor and intelligence. The fact that he could read and write benefited many who needed help with letters and business documents.

Abe aspired to public life, submitting his name for county representative in the Illinois legislature. Almost simultaneously, the Black Hawk War broke out and Abe enlisted. His all-volunteer company elected him Captain, and he served for eighty days, though he never faced combat. When he returned home, the campaign period was over, and he lost the election. Even though he had not campaigned, 277 out of 300 people in New Salem voted for him.

Yet, he continued along his chosen career path, privately studying law and arguing cases before the local court even before he passed the bar, earning his license in 1837. He remained active in the local political party, in opposition to President Andrew Jackson. Although Abe had campaigned for President Jackson's opponent, Jackson still

Wa-sáw-me-saw, Roaring Thunder, youngest son of Black Hawk

appointed him postmaster of New Salem. Since the job paid only $55 per year, he took extra work splitting rails, chopping wood, and advising on small legal cases.

In 1834, he was elected to the state legislature with a campaign strategy to shake hands and tell jokes. He won on likability and trust, and even voters in the opposing party voted for him. He served three consecutive terms thereafter.

Lincoln at his home on a horse

Moving On to Congress

In 1846, Lincoln ran for the U.S. House of Representatives. To secure the nomination, he promised his state party that he would not seek a second term. Once in Washington, he began opposing President Polk, denouncing the Mexican-American War by accusing Polk of dragging Americans into it on false pretenses. Perhaps he felt safe to voice an unpopular opinion, since he had no plans to run for re-election. In 1849, he went back home and practiced law.

From 1849 to 1856, Lincoln travelled the state becoming one of its most successful lawyers, while enduring the death of his 3-year-old son, Edward, in 1850. In 1858, he won his party's nomination for the U.S. Senate, challenging the current Senator, Stephen A. Douglas, who was up for re-election. In accepting the nomination, Lincoln delivered his "House Divided" speech, which many historians rank as the most important in all American history.

Notably, Lincoln challenged Douglas by stating that the greatest threat to American democracy was the "popular sovereignty" ideology—developed by Senator Douglas himself—which claimed that the issue of slavery should be resolved within each state. Lincoln countered with a bold assertion that slavery was immoral and should be dealt with by the U.S. Congress.

Attracting National Interest for the Lincoln-Douglas Debates

Consequently, they began a series of statewide debates, arousing intense national interest. Journalists from around the country followed them and published reports. No local election had ever won such national attention.

Lincoln lost to Douglas. But the debates garnered him national recognition. In the presidential campaign of 1860, two candidates represented the Republicans and Democrats. Two additional candidates were chosen by two parties that had splintered off. The unprecedented choice of four candidates was testimony to the shrieking-hot divisiveness in the nation.

Facing Down Secessionists

As President-elect, Abraham Lincoln waited three and a half months for his inauguration. During that time, seven states protested his election by seceding from the union. They formed the Confederate States of America and elected their own president, claiming that they had a right to revolt.

To which President Lincoln replied with a legal, logical argument. He explained that the "right" to revolt is not a legal one, but a moral one. And that morally, the right was only justified when civil rights and freedoms had been violated. He asked what rights of theirs had been violated by his election? And finally, he stated that revolution without a moral cause is "simply a wicked exercise of physical power."

Stephen Douglas

On his first day in office, President Lincoln received a request for supplies from Fort Sumter in Charleston, South Carolina. President Lincoln sent an unarmed supply ship, then notified President Davis of the Confederacy that it would be approaching the fort. Whereupon President Davis ordered an attack on the fort before the supplies could reach it. On the morning of April 12, 1861, the Confederacy fired on Fort Sumter, the first shots of the Civil War. For Lincoln, it was to be both a public trial and a deeply personal one, after the death of his second son William (11) in 1862.

Preserving the Union During the Civil War

President Lincoln's primary goal was to preserve the Union. It was not, at first, to free the enslaved. He thought the greater need was to keep four more "slave" states from seceding (Delaware, Kentucky, Maryland, and Missouri). Furthermore, the Constitution as he read it, did not allow the federal government to end slavery.

Civil War Naval Officers, unfinished portrait

However, early in the war, the need to free the enslaved population became obvious.

President Lincoln approached the loyal "slave" states with a proposal: The government would pay them the value of their enslaved persons, if they would free them. All refused. Lincoln realized then, that no slaveowner would voluntarily free his enslaved persons.

Additionally, once the war started, the enslaved Southern population began to run for the North. Moreover, Northern freedmen and white abolitionists pressured Lincoln to free them.

As a result, President Lincoln issued The Emancipation Proclamation, freeing all enslaved persons within the rebellion states. It earned him the title, The Great Emancipator. The work of preserving the civil rights of the newly freed was yet to come.

Ending the Civil War

On April 9, 1865 Union General Ulysses S. Grant accepted the surrender of Confederate General Robert E. Lee. As a sign of respect, Confederate officers were allowed to keep their swords. Five days later, a Southern sympathizer shot President Lincoln while he watched a play at Ford's Theatre. He never regained consciousness and died the next day.*

The Presidential Footprint

In 1986, the *Chicago Tribune* sent a survey to historians, including a list of desirable presidential qualities: leadership, crisis management and accomplishments, political skills, and personal character among others. The historians were asked to rate all presidents based on these qualities. In every category, Abraham Lincoln came out on top. His two greatest accomplishments, they agreed, were the preservation of the Union and the abolishment of slavery. They agreed that no one could have accomplished these two great works without Lincoln's keen intelligence, or his deep sense of morality, combined with an extraordinary political ability to manage a crisis environment. He remains our greatest president.

*For comprehension and vocabulary work, as well as mini-lessons on the National Banking system and the second inaugural address, see the *Discussion Guide*, pages 26-29.

Birth: February 12, 1809   **Place:** Hardin County, Kentucky   **Occupation:** Lawyer

Religion: No formal affiliation   **Term of Office:** 1861 to 1865   **Death:** April 15, 1865

Position on Slavery: He never owned any slaves, nor did his father.

Andrew Johnson

Growing Up on the Frontier

In 1808, Andrew Johnson was born in a log cabin in North Carolina to parents who were uneducated and could not read or write with any confidence. When he was fourteen, they apprenticed him to a tailor. This usually required the young person to live in the master's house and work for him for about seven years before the apprentice would be released. However, before his time was up, young Andrew ran away.

After a time, he returned to his mother's home, and the family moved to Greenville, Tennessee, where Andrew set up his own tailor shop at the age of seventeen. Andrew had not received any education at all during his childhood. But now in Greenville, he met Eliza McCardle, fell in love, and she taught him to read and write.

17th President of the United States

Entering the Public Sphere

They married and settled down in Greenville, where Andrew eventually became Mayor of the town. He also served in the state legislature and later was elected Governor of Tennessee. After serving a four-year term, he was selected to be a U.S. Senator representing Tennessee in Washington. When Southerners began talking of secession, Senator Johnson strongly opposed it. He may have identified with the tradesmen of his state, rather than with the planter class whom he considered to be spoiled elites.

To unite the country, President Lincoln chose him to be his Vice President for his re-election campaign in 1864. A southern senator who supported slavery but not secession would be the perfect bridge between the parties. They won a landslide victory. Yet on April 14, 1865, Lincoln was assassinated and died the next day. Andrew Johnson took the oath of office on April 15.

Accepting the Demands of the Hour

President Johnson was an experienced politician; however, he was not prepared for the excruciating task of post-Civil War reconciliation with the South. And although he had been pitted against the southern planter class during his working years as a tailor, some historians think he might have been eager to have them show him respect in his new position.

While Congress was in recess from April through December of that year, President Johnson worked swiftly to push through his own Reconstruction plans. He quickly delivered thousands of pardons, and in just a few months, most of the elite enslavers were back in power at the state level. They, in turn, rapidly set up "black codes"—laws that restricted the rights of the newly freed black population.

Swimming Against the Tide

When Congress returned in December of that year, they voted not to accept the newly established southern states' representatives, or to recognize their constitutions as valid. During the next few years, Johnson and Congress battled unendingly over plans for Reconstruction. By 1867, Congress passed legislation to limit the President's powers and voted to impeach him. Though he was saved from removal by one vote. After leading an angry and resentful campaign, President Johnson lost his bid for re-election in 1868.*

The Presidential Footprint

During the second half of the twentieth century, many historians have judged President Johnson's tenure to be a grossly unfortunate episode in American history. They point out that his policies maintained the sectional differences in the country and did nothing to heal them.

*For comprehension and vocabulary work, see the *Discussion Guide*, page 30.

Birth: December 29, 1808 **Place:** Raleigh, North Carolina **Occupation:** Tailor; Public Servant

Religion: No formal affiliation **Term of Office:** 1865 to 1869 **Death:** July 31, 1875

Position on Slavery: He was a tradesman who held a few enslaved persons.

- Before the war, he was a firm supporter of slavery.

- He disagreed strongly with the South's secession.

- In August 1863, he freed his slaves in accordance with the Emancipation Proclamation.

Ulysses S. Grant

Escaping from the Tannery

Ulysses was the oldest of six children born to a leather tanner and his wife. His dad treated animal hides to be turned into usable leather for products like saddles, shoes, and belts. When Ulysses was little, he helped his dad, but the chemicals smelled so bad that Ulysses swore to never become a tanner.

Instead, he had an unusual talent for horsemanship. He was such a natural, that his father applied to the United States Military Academy at West Point for him. In those days, the cavalry was a big part of the army because many troops rode horses into battle.

Accepting a Military Life

At first, when Ulysses learned that he was accepted, he was shocked and didn't want to go. But he eventually decided that it was a good education that his father would never be able to afford. So, he took the deal—a free education in exchange for a promise of military service.

18th President of the United States

Upon graduation and despite his remarkable horsemanship, Ulysses was assigned to the Fourth Infantry. They were foot soldiers at Jefferson Barracks, south of St. Louis. In his first deployment to the Mexican War, he served as a lieutenant under General Zachary Taylor, often admiring his calm leadership. As time moved on, he also served in Detroit, New York, the Oregon Territory, and California.

Early in the Civil War, Grant proved his worth by scoring significant victories in Missouri and Tennessee, thereby catching President Lincoln's attention. In 1863, Grant was put in command of the siege of Vicksburg, Mississippi. He stood firm and took the city, thus turning the tide in the North's favor. His soldiers were amazed at his calm demeanor in battle. He knew how to give orders, then back off and let the soldiers do the job.

In recognition of Grant's value, President Lincoln made him Lieutenant General and Commander of all the Union forces. By the end of the war, he was General of the Armies, the only man other than George Washington to hold that position.

Stepping into the Presidency

In 1869, President Grant's top priority was preserving the newly freed Black Americans' civil rights. Even Northerners at that time did not support full civil rights for them, yet the Fourteenth Amendment had given the freed slaves citizenship status (1866). Next, Congress proposed the Fifteenth Amendment, which gave all citizens the right to vote, regardless of any previous condition of servitude. Grant urged its passage and signed it into law in 1870.

To protect their new rights, President Grant signed the Ku Klux Klan Act in 1871. They were a group that had formed to intimidate the new freed men and women through violence. Grant acted to enforce the law several months later by sending troops into the South to restore order where terrorism against Black Americans had been active.

Perhaps because of General Grant's experiences touring the West with the army, he was committed to changing American policy toward Native Americans. He appointed the first non-white Commissioner of Indian Affairs, Brigadier General Ely S. Parker, a Seneca Indian. Grant also set up a Board of Indian Commissioners run by civic leaders who were active in charitable organizations.*

The Presidential Footprint

Although General Grant was a remarkably successful battlefield leader, he was not a successful President. He admitted that he did not like politics, and this distaste may have prevented him from engaging in some of the negotiations that would have brought him more success in the office. However, historians more recently have given him credit for fighting for Black American civil rights more than any other president of the nineteenth century.

*For comprehension and vocabulary work, see the *Discussion Guide*, page 31.

Birth: April 27, 1822 **Place:** Point Pleasant, Ohio **Occupation:** Soldier

Religion: Methodist **Term of Office:** 1869 to 1877 **Death:** July 23, 1885

Position on Slavery and Civil Rights: His family never enslaved anyone, although his wife's family did.

- During a short term as a farmer, he hired freedmen to work his farm.
- His father-in-law gave him one enslaved person.
- During a period of extreme poverty, he could have sold the enslaved person to get some income, but Grant freed him instead.

Rutherford B. Hayes

Facing Tragedy and Poverty in Childhood

Rutherford B. Hayes was a sickly child, cared for by a single mother and older sister who nicknamed him Rud. His father had died a few months before his birth, and to make ends meet, his mother rented out rooms. When Rud was two, his nine-year-old brother drowned. His mother appealed to her brother for help, and Uncle Sardis, who was a prosperous businessman, became an affectionate father figure for Rud.

Though his mother taught him to read and write, by age nine, he attended a local school run by Daniel Granger, a colorful teacher who ruled the class with frontier knife-throwing skills. Rud recalled that Granger once expertly threw a knife inches away from the head of a boy who had leaned over to talk to him. Before long, Rud escaped Granger and went to a private school, paid for by Uncle Sardis. He continued to Kenyon College in Ohio and then finished at Harvard Law School.

19th President of the United States

Defending Northern Causes

As a lawyer, he successfully defended a young black girl against her enslaver. In 1855, her owner had taken the girl through Ohio, a free state, on the way to Virginia when an anti-slavery group took her case to court. Her owner appeared in court and asked whether she would choose to stay with him, or freedom. When she chose freedom, he had her arrested as a runaway. In a later hearing, Hayes successfully defended her, and the young girl was freed.

At 40 years old, Hayes fought for the North in the Civil War. He was wounded twice. But both times, he went back into action where he led several important battles and was eventually promoted to brigadier general.

Before the war ended, his friends nominated him for a position in the U.S. House of Representatives. They wanted him to come home and campaign, to which he responded, "An officer fit for duty who at this crisis would abandon his post to electioneer for a seat in Congress ought to be scalped. You may feel perfectly sure I shall do no such thing." He was elected on the strength of that statement, without doing any campaigning.

While in Congress he supported the passage of the 14th and 15th Amendments, which gave citizenship and voting rights to newly freed Black Americans. In 1867, he was elected Governor of Ohio and led the state to ratify the 15th Amendment to the U.S. Constitution.

Dealing in the Back Rooms for the Presidency

He won the presidency in the Compromise of 1877, one of the murkiest deals in U.S. history. With emotional wounds still aching from the war, Americans voted in 1876 for either Hayes, the Governor of Ohio, or Samuel Tilden, Governor of New York. After many weeks of counting ballots, the outcome rested on tallies in Oregon, Florida, Louisiana, and South Carolina. In the end, Hayes won by 1 electoral vote, even though Tilden had won the popular vote.

In his inaugural address, President Hayes pledged to equally guard the civil rights of both the whites and the newly freed black citizens in the South. However, the southern Democrats had fought and won state control across the South, often with the help of homegrown terrorist groups like the Ku Klux Klan, except in Louisiana and South Carolina. In both of those states, small regiments of federal troops guarded the Republican-led state houses.

Ending the Reconstruction of the South

In Washington, D.C., the Democratic-run House refused to fund the army while federal troops remained in the South. Hayes was forced to remove them. His only leverage was to pressure promises from southern democrats that they would guard civil rights for Black Americans. Yet since the Democrats had regained complete control of the South, they broke their promises.

The Presidential Footprint

Though many historians in the past had blamed Hayes for ending Reconstruction of the South, today historians recognize that Reconstruction was mostly over before Hayes took office. The recent consensus is that Hayes was the last president of his century to have fought actively to protect Black Americans' civil rights.

*For comprehension and vocabulary work, see the *Discussion Guide*, page 32.

Birth: October 4, 1822   **Place:** Delaware, Ohio   **Occupation:** Lawyer

Religion: Methodist   **Term of Office:** 1877 to 1881   **Death:** January 17, 1893

Position on Slavery and Civil Rights: His family did not enslave anyone.

- His wife's family inherited a few enslaved persons.
- When faced with poverty and urged to sell their enslaved people, his mother-in-law declared that she would take in washing before making money from such a sale.
- He had been a moderate abolitionist but was influenced by his wife's strong anti-slavery politics.

James A. Garfield

Trying Out Farming and Canal Work

James A. Garfield was born in Ohio and never knew his father. He had died shortly after James was born, leaving him to a hardscrabble life with his widowed mother. The small family lived on a farm on the Ohio frontier, a single mother with three children. His father had been known for his physical strength, and young James seemed to take after him, so he was helpful on the farm.

The hard work made him realize that he did not like farming, and he left at age sixteen to get a job on the canal boats, carrying loads between Pittsburgh and Cleveland. In only six weeks, he fell off the boat fourteen times. He finally got sick and went home.

20th President of the United States

Getting an Education

For his second attempt to leave the farm, he worked several part-time jobs while attending school. He was a carpenter, a part-time teacher, and a janitor—all while studying. When he was eighteen, he joined his parents' church and became a sincere, active member. Early on, he identified as a reformer and supported the abolitionist cause. At age twenty-three, he enrolled as a junior in Williams College in western Massachusetts, from which he graduated with honors in 1856.

Teaching at a Church-Centered College

His first job was teaching at the Eclectic Institute, a church-centered college in Ohio, where he eventually became a minister and its President. But in his first years there, he turned to politics, supporting John C. Fremont for Governor. But by 1861, he had passed the bar exam and left the college. He had been elected to the state legislature as one of its youngest members.

When the Civil War broke out, James helped establish the 42nd Ohio Infantry, earning military honors when he gained control of eastern Kentucky for the Union in a battle in which his troops were heavily outnumbered. In another battle, he rode skillfully in the open under heavy enemy fire. His achievements were awarded with quick advances to Lieutenant Colonel. The public took notice and elected him to the U. S. House of Representatives, without him ever campaigning for the job. He had to resign from the military to accept the seat in Congress.

Serving in Congress

Congressman James A. Garfield quickly aligned with the most Radical Republicans in Washington. During his eight terms he softened a bit, even advising forgiveness for some of the defeated Southerners. He served on influential committees in Congress, such as Chairman of the Appropriations Committee, responsible for disbursing funds to all the government agencies.

After the controversial election of 1876, he was on the committee to investigate the disputed electoral college votes from Oregon, South Carolina, Florida, and Louisiana. In fact, he was a member of the committee that gave Rutherford B. Hayes the contested election and removed the last of the Union military from the South.

Winning with the Electoral College

James A. Garfield won the 1880 election by only 7,368 popular votes, although he won the electoral college by 59 votes. While he spent about seventeen years in Congress, he was only President for 100 days. Inaugurated on March 4, he was shot in September and died about five days later.

He had spent most of those 100 days appointing his cabinet, paying special attention to the Port of New York. The manager in charge of that port was in a unique position to skim money off the taxes collected with every ship's unloading. President Garfield replaced the current manager, who was known as a reformer, with someone to whom he owed a political favor.*

The Presidential Footprint

Many historians agree that President Garfield was not in office long enough to have made much of an impact on government, or in American history. They point to his replacement of the reformer in the Port of New York offices as perhaps a hint of what may have come. In that case, some historians think that his record in Congress was a better one to end his career on.

*For comprehension and vocabulary work, as well as a mini-lesson on Jim Crow laws, see the *Discussion Guide*, pages 33-34.

Birth: November 19, 1831   **Place:** Cuyahoga County, Ohio   **Occupation:** Teacher, Public Official

Religion: Disciples of Christ   **Term of Office:** 1881   **Death:** September 19, 1881

Position on Civil Rights: James Garfield was a committed abolitionist, and his family never enslaved any persons.

- As a Congressman after the Civil War, he supported the passage of the 13th, 14th, and 15th Amendments, which made Black Americans free, gave them citizenship, and allowed adult black males to vote.

- As Jim Crow laws took effect, Garfield spoke out against "those dreadful scenes enacted by the Ku Klux organization." He condemned them as "shocking barbarities."

Chester A. Arthur

Pulling Himself Up by the Bootstraps

President Chester A. Arthur earned his nickname, "The Dude," in reference to his love of expensive clothing, extravagant partying, and a White House renovation totaling $2 million (in today's money). But he was born in a log cabin in Vermont, the son of a fierce abolitionist Baptist preacher. During his childhood, his father moved the family several times, from one congregation to the next. He learned to read and write at home before entering Union College in 1845, as a seventeen-year-old sophomore.

After college, he read law and taught school. His ambitions reflected a vision that would take him far away from his modest childhood home. He dreamed of becoming a wealthy lawyer in New York City. When he passed the bar exam in 1854, his father tapped his connections to get Chester a job clerking at a prestigious law firm, known for handling civil rights cases.

21st President of the United States

Supporting the Union

When the Civil War started, Arthur enlisted with the New York militia and became the Quartermaster General, in charge of ordering supplies, and housing the troops. He developed into a crack administrator and earned the rank of brigadier general.

He never saw combat but was not disappointed, since his wife was a Southerner, with relatives fighting for the Confederacy. He retired from the military in 1863 and went back to his law practice, specializing in clients who were suing for war-related damages. He became wealthy and caught the attention of a powerful New York City political boss, who made him chief counsel for the NYC Tax Commission.

In 1871, President Ulysses S. Grant appointed him Collector of the Port of New York. This was the ripest patronage job of the period. Because nearly 75% of the taxes that the U.S. government collected came through this port, from taxation on foreign goods entering the country. It was an office where bribes were often exchanged, and skimming money from the till was common. The job was usually given as a reward to someone who had helped elect the governor, or President.

Earning a Patronage Job from the Election of 1880

The New York City political machine was very powerful in that era. As a reward for his service, they recommended Chester A. Arthur for Vice President. Although James

Garfield was not happy with the appointment, at the time, he could not refuse. He won the election, and Arthur, having never won a political election, was suddenly in politics.

What's more, in only 100 days, upon the death of President Garfield, Chester A. Arthur took the oath of office and became President.

Bearing the Shock of the Presidency

At first, the Washington political world was very worried about Arthur taking the helm. But he surprised everyone by proving to be a very competent administrator. His work as quartermaster general and manager of the Port of New York turned out to have been a solid training ground.

What surprised most people was that he signed the Pendleton Civil Service Reform Act, which made it illegal to give government jobs to people as rewards for political help. He also vetoed the first-round Chinese Exclusion Act, against his party's wishes. In addition, as a move toward modernization, he authorized the spending for some new steel ocean cruisers and earned the title from historians as the "Father of the Steel Navy."*

The Presidential Footprint

It is entirely possible that President Chester A. Arthur surprised his friends and enemies because he knew that he was dying of the fatal Bright's Disease. He had been diagnosed in 1882 and died shortly after leaving office. Today, many historians point to Chester A. Arthur as a significant fulcrum between the post-Civil War era and America's entrance into the modern world.

*For comprehension and vocabulary work, see the *Discussion Guide*, page 35.

Birth: October 5, 1829 **Place:** Fairfield, Vermont **Occupation:** Lawyer

Religion: Episcopalian **Term of Office:** 1881 - 1885 **Death:** November 18, 1886

Position on Civil Rights and Immigration: As a young lawyer, Arthur defended a black woman who was kicked off a New York streetcar. He won, forcing the railroad companies to seat all riders fairly.

- About 2,000 Black Americans held public office in the early years after the Civil War, including sixteen men in the U.S. House of Representatives.

- In 1881, when Arthur became President, suppression of the Black vote in the South was just beginning.

- President Arthur vetoed the Chinese Exclusion Act, a twenty-year ban against Chinese immigration, speaking favorably about Chinese influence on the American economy. However, he signed the second version with a ten-year ban.

Grover Cleveland

Serving Two Non-Consecutive Terms

Grover Cleveland never intended to become a politician. Yet, he was the only president in history to serve two non-consecutive terms as president. When he won his first election, it was because he was truly an outsider.

Relying on His Astonishing Memory

He was born as the middle of nine children to a poor Presbyterian minister and his wife. He grew up in central New York State, and at age sixteen his father died. Grover immediately went to work to support his family, letting go of his dreams for college. He and his brother worked, and he eventually took a law clerk job and became a law student. Without ever having gone to college, he passed the bar exam and became a lawyer in 1858.

22nd and 24th President of the United States

When the Civil War broke out, he spent $300 to hire a replacement for himself and continued working as a lawyer. He had an astounding memory, delivering all his opening and closing arguments before the jury without notes.

Earning His First Elected Office

His first elected office came directly from his reputation as a great lawyer, when he won the election for sheriff of Erie County, New York. Throughout his one-year term, and perhaps inspired by his love for the law, he became a reformer who uncovered and cleaned up corruption, without regard for political loyalties.

So, when the political organization asked him to run for mayor of Buffalo, he was surprised, but accepted. He won the post and continued cleaning up corruption in the city services departments. In that era, political corruption and the need for reform was a focus of many elections. Voters liked what they saw in Cleveland and sent him straight to the Governor's mansion in Albany.

From there, he tackled the NYC corruption without hesitation, ignoring the politicians who had helped him get elected. His reputation as a reformer carried him straight to the White House, and he took the oath of office in 1885.

Carrying the Vision of a Reformer

As Cleveland took office, he carried into the White House the heart of a city-street reformer. He adopted a watchdog mentality that policed Congress and stopped any bills that seemed to award political favors or spend excess money. Although he was acting in the manner for which he had been elected, he did not have a sense of the Presidency as a visionary leader. He acted as a sheriff and a prosecutor. For example, he vetoed hundreds of requests for army pensions because he thought they were fraudulent.

In 1893, President Grover Cleveland took the oath of office for the second time, during the worst economic depression in U.S. history up to that time. Up to 25% of urban factory workers were unemployed. One-tenth of all banks had closed, and almost 50% of railroad construction had stopped.

But the worst event was the walk-out of 150,000 railroad workers. They were supporting the Pullman railroad employees, largely Black Americans. These workers had received a pay cut along with a rent increase in the company town outside of Chicago that they were required to live in. Rail service around the country halted.

President Cleveland, who had previously stated he did not believe that it was the government's job to intervene in social issues, nevertheless, sent in the military to force the workers to end the strike. Many Americans were alarmed at the use of Presidential force, especially because the Governor of Illinois specifically told him he did not want the army.*

The Presidential Footprint

Most historians do not think that Cleveland was a good president. His accomplishments were positive moves in civil service reform. Yet, he did not have a leadership vision in his dealings with Congress. He explained that in being above party politics, he had a direct relationship with his electorate, which is a monarch's view of leadership, and not a president's role. However, other historians point out that since he so freely vetoed bills, he re-established an appropriate balance between the legislative and the executive branches of government.

*For comprehension and vocabulary questions as well as a mini lesson on political machines, see the *Discussion Guide*, pages 36-37.

Birth: March 18, 1837   **Place:** Caldwell, New Jersey   **Occupation:** Lawyer

Religion: Presbyterian   **Term of Office:** 1885 to 1889 and 1893 to 1897   **Death:** June 24, 1908

Position on Civil Rights: He opposed integrating schools in New York State and supported white Southerners in their resistance to treat Black Americans as equals.

- President Cleveland did not think that "social problems" were within the scope of the federal government and opposed any congressional action to cancel Jim Crow laws.

- He encouraged Native Americans to accept European customs.

- He did not speak either in favor of or against women's suffrage.

Benjamin Harrison

Inheriting a Legacy of Public Service

President Benjamin Harrison was called "the human iceberg" behind his back by White House staff. He was overly formal, never expressing any warmth toward his coworkers, and he quit working at noon each day to play with his grandchildren. One day he chased their pet goat down Pennsylvania Avenue as it ran away with the cart his grandson rode in. When he failed to win re-election, he said it felt like he was let out of prison. So why did he ever run for office?

Young Benjamin was keenly aware of his esteemed political heritage: His great-grandfather was Colonel Benjamin Harrison, a signer of the Declaration of Independence. Moreover, his grandfather was President William Henry Harrison, and his father served in the U.S. House of Representatives. His heritage overshadowed his childhood love of fishing, hunting, and tending to his family's livestock. He had private tutors before enrolling in Farmers College and later Miami University, from which he graduated with honors.

23rd President of the United States

Choosing a Political Life

He enjoyed spending quiet time in his grandfather's library, whose home was not far away. Perhaps because he felt close to his grandfather, he thought that he too was destined for politics. After college he became a lawyer, married, and moved to Indianapolis, where he set up his law practice, working there from 1856 to 1860.

Almost immediately he jumped into politics, winning election to city attorney. He was soon secretary of the Republican State Central Committee, supporting Abraham Lincoln for President. Furthermore, he later worked for the Supreme Court of Indiana, supervising the publication of all the Court's decisions.

In 1862, he enlisted for the Union and served under General Sherman during his march across the South that ended with the burning of Atlanta. He did not feel proud of his military service. Although he served with honor, "foresight, discipline and a fighting spirit," according to Major General Sherman, he nevertheless keenly felt the torment of warfare and was relieved when he retired in 1865.

Turning back to politics, he failed twice to win the governorship of Indiana. But he was appointed to a national commission by President Rutherford B. Hayes, putting him finally in the national spotlight. This led to an appointment as U.S. Senator from Indiana, from 1881 to 1887. In Congress, he fought hard to gain pensions for Civil War veterans, for a modernized navy, and for the preservation of wilderness lands.

Taking on the Presidency

In 1889, President Benjamin Harrison took the oath of office. Perhaps he was tired after nearly thirty years in politics, but he was not easy to work with—stiff and unnecessarily formal. And he quit working every day at noon.

Yet he did pass a few important laws. One was the Sherman Antitrust Act, which forced large corporations to break into smaller businesses. It was an effort to keep the very wealthy businessmen from keeping prices high, and from paying their workers too little. At first, the law was weak and did not have much effect, but it was important. So, as the years went by, future presidents strengthened it, creating a powerful tool in use throughout the next century.

Another law that President Harrison supported was the Force Bill. It would have given the federal government supervision over congressional elections in southern states, so newly freed Black Americans could vote. Although congressional supporters and President Benjamin Harrison campaigned hard for its passage, they failed. However, President Harrison also backed and won the passage of the Land Revision Act, establishing the first national park in Yellowstone, Wyoming.*

The Presidential Footprint

Until the 1960s, most historians rated President Benjamin Harrison as mediocre, not the worst though not great either. But in recent decades, historians are reconsidering his contribution. They point to his support for expanding the Navy into a small fleet of steel-armored ships, begun by President Arthur. It proved to be a foundation for Theodore Roosevelt's commitment to a modern ocean-going military force.

*For comprehension and vocabulary work, see the *Discussion Guide*, page 38.

Birth: August 20, 1833   **Place:** North Bend, Ohio   **Occupation:** Lawyer

Religion: Presbyterian   **Term of Office:** 1889 to1893   **Death:** March 13, 1901

Position on Civil Rights and Immigration: He opposed his party by refusing to support the Chinese Exclusion Act of 1882.

- He vigorously campaigned on behalf of two bills meant to protect civil rights for Black Americans. He also faithfully enforced the 15th Amendment and appointed Frederick Douglass U.S. Minister to Haiti.

- He said the government had "an obligation solemn as a covenant with God to save [freedmen] from the dastardly outrages that their rebel masters are committing upon them in the South."

William McKinley

Valuing Prayer, Honesty, and Hard Work

William McKinley was born in a small Ohio town and had a happy childhood with a devout mother who taught him the value of prayer and honesty. His father owned an iron foundry and demonstrated a strong work ethic that William imitated. He was a good student who valued his education in a Methodist school. He attended college for one semester and then dropped out for lack of finances.

25th President of the United States

At the outbreak of the Civil War, he enlisted in the 23rd Ohio Volunteer Infantry, where his superiors noted that the young private fought well at the Battle of Antietam. Later, he was promoted to second lieutenant under Colonel Rutherford B. Hayes, who mentored William. They maintained their relationship throughout their military years and beyond. He made it up to brevet major, a battlefield promotion, and kept the title throughout his career.

Entering the Public Space

After the war, McKinley attended Albany Law School and by 1869, he was elected county prosecutor. By 1876, he was a member of the U.S. Congress where he served until 1891. He became influential in Congress, chairing the powerful House Ways and Means Committee. This committee's job is to answer the question: How will the government accomplish its goals? How will they be paid for? The answer lay in taxes and tariffs, or taxes on imported goods.

So, committee member McKinley drafted the McKinley Tariff of 1890. It was a powerful law that raised the price of consumer goods, including imports. But the public did not distinguish between domestic and imported goods and was angry over increased prices. McKinley lost his next election and went home, where he was elected Governor of Ohio. There, he managed disputes between labor and management in an era that saw endless strikes. Most people thought he was a competent manager, and he won re-election.

Fixing on Gold in the Presidency

Since the early days of the United States, Congress had used a monetary system that relied on foreign silver coins. In 1792, the U.S. adopted a bimetal standard, meaning that it backed its paper money with both silver and gold. The government debated endlessly between commitment to a gold or silver standard in nearly every election.

Yet, it was not just an American decision because it affected international trade as well. But by 1897, no other foreign trading partner would agree to a bimetal system.

So, President McKinley signed the Gold Standard Act in 1900, placing the U.S. on a gold standard. It would become a factor in the Great Depression only thirty years away.

In addition, the outbreak of the Spanish-American War launched the United States into imperialism, or governance of foreign territories. This was hotly debated on the home front, and President McKinley's role in it is still debated today.

Finally, the President faced the country's still tender Civil War memories against growing difficulties that Black Americans faced in the South, as Jim Crow* laws steadily took hold. President McKinley showed support for Black Americans by giving a speech at a Black American church, and visiting the Tuskegee Institute, a black college. But he was unable to pass any laws to protect the newly freed Black Americans.

He did not have security in the early days of constant contact with the public—with tragic consequences. A gunman approached and shot him at a public event on September 6, 1901. He died eight days later.*

The Presidential Footprint

Because President McKinley served during a transition period in American history, historians have debated his place in the changes that took decades to evolve. However, scholars today tend to agree that in navigating difficult waters, McKinley set the precedent for inviting journalists to regular briefings. He seemed to understand the value of mailing information out to keep the public informed about his policies and decisions. In this way, he ushered in the modern era of the presidential press briefings and public speaking.

*For comprehension and vocabulary work, see the *Discussion Guide*, page 39.

Birth: January 29, 1843   **Place:** Niles, Ohio   **Occupation:** Lawyer

Religion: Methodist   **Term of Office:** 1897 to 1901   **Death:** September 14, 1901

Position on Civil Rights and Immigration: As lynch mobs grew more common, more than 100 per year, President McKinley condemned them in his inauguration speech, though he did not follow through with legal action during his term of office.

- President McKinley was on friendly terms with George Henry White, the only Black congressman in Washington from 1897 to 1901.

- He appointed about thirty Black Americans to government positions.

Theodore Roosevelt

Overcoming Childhood Illnesses

Although Theodore Roosevelt was the first President to use the media to project his image to the country, his extrovert personality was not created only for, or by, the media. His tendency toward energetic endeavor was present as a child.

Oddly, young "Teddie" was a sickly child who struggled with sports because of asthma. By his teen years, he attacked his problem with a vigorous weight-lifting routine, and he took pride in the physique he acquired. From then on, he was a great advocate of outdoor living and adventure, taking on wrestling, boxing, hiking, horseback riding, and swimming.

Facing Early Success and Tragedy

His father was a wealthy businessman and philanthropist, while his mother had been raised on a Southern plantation. So Teddie grew up in luxury and had tutors who came to his home in Oyster Bay, New York, on Long Island. The family traveled the world throughout the late 1860s and 1870's, but they were home by 1876 when Teddy enrolled in Harvard. He displayed an energetic intellectual interest in many subjects, and studied languages, sciences, and English rhetoric, or the art of argumentation or persuasion.

Upon graduation, he married his college sweetheart and attended one year of law school. However, he decided he didn't like the law, so he entered politics and

26th President of the United States

Theodore Roosevelt as a young assemblyman

was elected to two terms in the New York Assembly. Though life seemed to be going smoothly, shortly after giving birth to their first child, his wife died of kidney disease. Tragically, his mother died in the same week of typhoid fever.

Overcoming Grief

Plunged into grief, Theodore tried for a short while to throw himself into his work. But after several weeks, he left his newborn daughter in the care of his sister and traveled to the Dakotas, where he bought a ranch and immersed himself for over a year in the cowboy and ranching lifestyle—cattle herding, riding, and hunting. He had a reformer's spirit that seemed to others in the West that he was untouched by grief. He even tried out a stint as a western sheriff.

Theodore Roosevelt when he was a New York police commissioner

But by 1886 he had remarried, a childhood sweetheart, and settled back into the Eastern lifestyle. He moved his family to Oyster Bay, New York and went back to writing and politics. He wrote two biographies of famous Americans, and four volumes that chronicled the settling of the West.

He also energetically campaigned for presidential candidate Benjamin Harrison. The New York political machine rewarded him with a job at the U.S. Civil Service Commission, and he later accepted an offer to be President of the New York City Police Board. He proved to be more honest in the political work than the political machine had hoped, as they watched him vigorously clean up corruption in its offices. The political bosses were surprised at his reformer inclinations, aimed at them and their co-workers, and unhappy with his record.

Leading the Rough Riders

In 1897, President McKinley appointed him as Secretary of the Navy. When the Spanish-American War broke out, he resigned so he could organize a regiment of volunteer cavalry, called the Rough Riders. They made headlines when Theodore Roosevelt led the charge up Kettle Hill in support of the capture of San Juan Hill and battle victory.

As a war hero, he won the election for Governor of New York, but he refused to follow the party bosses' practice of ignoring corruption. So to get rid of him, the New York political machine put him on the national ticket as Vice President to William McKinley.

Though the Rough Riders did charge up a nearby hill, in support of the Battle of San Juan Hill, it was not San Juan Hill, as this painting depicts.

Succeeding McKinley

Theodore Roosevelt took the oath of office upon McKinley's assassination. It was September 1901, and he promised the nation to continue with McKinley's programs. Although he was true to his word, as his tenure progressed, he realized that he wanted to earn the presidency in his own right in the next election.

President Theodore Roosevelt was the first President who thought that it was the federal government's job to work on behalf of the people—in particular, to protect them from corporate greed. One of his first acts was to sue a large group of railroad businesses called Northern Securities Company, seeking to break up that monopoly. The government won its case and forced the monopoly to dissolve.

Next, Roosevelt decided to strengthen the role of the Interstate Commerce Commission by giving it authority to regulate interstate shipping rates. At the time, large companies got cheaper rates than smaller businesses, and President Roosevelt sought to give small businesses a fair chance at better prices.

When Congress resisted, Roosevelt took his case directly to the people. He toured the nation making speeches, applying pressure to Congress, until they passed the landmark Hepburn Act, strengthening the ability of the Interstate Commerce Commission to set fair rates for businesses of all sizes.*

The Presidential Footprint

President Theodore Roosevelt left a legacy of a strengthened Presidency. He balanced the Executive branch against the powerful Legislative branch, which had ruled the government throughout the nineteenth century. At the dawn of the twentieth, the presidency transformed the government into a more balanced institution.

Theodore Roosevelt and John Muir at Yosemite

President Roosevelt used his charismatic leadership, another first in American history, to steer the government toward social and economic justice. He intervened in a national coal strike that was about to hit the country right before winter. Although the President has no authority over private businesses, he called the striking parties to the White House for negotiations. He managed to steer the signing of what he called a Square Deal for all parties. It became the slogan for all his work as President, though it must be said that he did not extend that concept to Black Americans.

He also created 150 new national forests, 5 national parks, and 15 wildlife refuges. Historians generally consider President Theodore Roosevelt to be the first modern President. He is noted for being a charismatic leader, for carrying his causes to the people, and setting up presidential press conferences.

*For comprehension and vocabulary work, see the *Discussion Guide*, page 40-41.

Birth: October 27, 1858   **Place:** New York, New York   **Occupation:** Author, Lawyer, Public Official

Religion: Dutch Reformed   **Term of Office:** 1901 to 1909   **Death:** January 6, 1919

Position on Civil Rights and Immigration: Although President Roosevelt believed that some black persons were superior to some white persons, he did not believe on the whole that black Americans were equal to white Americans.

- He invited Black leader and educator Booker T. Washington to the White House. The Southern press severely chastised Roosevelt for which he was surprised but did not apologize.

- When a small group of black soldiers was accused of a killing spree in Texas, Roosevelt forced the dishonorable discharge of three black companies (160 soldiers) without trial.

William Howard Taft

Focusing on Academics and the Law

President William Howard Taft's lifelong dream was to be Chief Justice of the Supreme Court, which he attained after one term as President.

As a child, William excelled in academics and played baseball, graduating second in his high school class and enrolling in Yale. His father thought sports were a distraction, so William focused only on academics. He graduated once again second in his class and then enrolled in the University of Cincinnati Law School. Law was the only field that interested William.

27th President of the United States

He inherited this talent from his father, Alphonso Taft, who was the Secretary of War and later the Attorney General for President Ulysses S. Grant. His mother was socially active as an advocate for kindergarten in the school system. When William married, his wife encouraged him to follow his father's political path. Although he was content with his judicial roles, he accepted political appointments to please her.

Moving Toward the Supreme Court

For years, he moved up the judicial ladder—he was assistant prosecutor in Hamlin County, Ohio, and then became a judge of the Cincinnati Superior Court. But it was while he worked as U.S. Solicitor General in Washington, D.C. that he became friends with Theodore Roosevelt, who was also working in the government.

Later, he served on the Sixth U.S. Circuit Court of Appeals, hoping that it would be a path to the Supreme Court. But when he was summoned to Washington by President McKinley, it was for a position as Governor of the Philippine Islands, acquired from Spain in the Spanish-American War. He worried about taking the job, but his wife was thrilled. So, he took it and helped write their constitution, bill of rights, and other legal government documents. He was Governor of the Philippines, a position in the Executive branch, but he did the work that was more natural for him—setting up the documents for the Judicial branch.

It did exactly what his wife hoped; it made him the Secretary of War in President Theodore Roosevelt's cabinet. When President Roosevelt announced that he would not seek re-election, he nominated William Taft for the ticket. He reluctantly agreed and won, based on Roosevelt's enthusiastic public recommendation and Taft's promise to continue Roosevelt's policies.

Breaking Promises

Soon after he took office, voters worried that he would not keep his promise. The first alarm sounded when he signed a tariff bill, supposed to lessen taxes on imported goods. Instead, it did very little to change the prices. This satisfied businessmen because it kept U.S. goods cheaper than foreign goods. But Roosevelt loyalists were angry because the law made U.S. jobs less secure.

The second alarm rang when President Taft fired ex-President Roosevelt's Chief Forrester, Gifford Pinchot. Over Pinchot, President Taft appointed a businessman as Secretary of the Interior, who immediately opened tracts of national lands for industrial development that ex-President Roosevelt had preserved. Gifford Pinchot publicly objected to his boss's actions, and President Taft fired him.

For ex-President Roosevelt's followers, President Taft was a turncoat. The Republican Party was ablaze with arguments between the progressive and conservative wings. President Taft, though he may not have been too worried about it, had set himself up as a one-term President. In fact, the Republican Party was so divided that Roosevelt came back to run for a third term. His pull of half of the party votes split the Republican votes and handed the next Presidency over to Woodrow Wilson.*

The Presidential Footprint

Most Progressive politicians and the public complained about President Taft's perceived ineffectiveness. Yet many historians point out that he initiated more than 80 antitrust lawsuits during his term. He approached reform from the judicial branch, actions that were largely overlooked. Though a President and leader of the Executive branch, he approached his duties through the lens of the courts. Perhaps it was his natural point of view. As he said toward the end of his life: "I don't remember that I ever was President."

*For comprehension and vocabulary work, see the *Discussion Guide*, page 42.

Birth: September 15, 1857   **Place:** Cincinnati, Ohio   **Occupation:** Lawyer, Public Official

Religion: Unitarian   **Term of Office:** 1909 to 1913   **Death:** March 8, 1930

Position on Civil Rights and Immigration: Mrs. Taft initiated strict segregation among the White House staff. She ordered black and white servants to dine separately, with the approval of President Taft.

- As Chief Justice of the Supreme Court, William Taft wrote a dissenting opinion supporting the right of Congress to make laws that correct a "recognizable evil." In this case, it was a minimum wage law meant to protect women and children.

World War I

This biplane seats two and was used as a bomber during World War I. It was a British design. But it was built in America because when the U.S. entered the war, it did not have any suitable planes for combat.

Gas masks were worn by soldiers to protect against bombs filled with poisonous mustard gas.

Women were encouraged to take work formerly only deemed acceptable for men, in order to support the war effort.

The government needed to raise money quickly to purchase war supplies: transportation, arms, munitions, and uniforms. They used posters like this one to encourage the public to buy Liberty Bonds to raise funds.

Woodrow Wilson

Growing Up During the Civil War

Woodrow Wilson was born in the South and grew up during the Civil War. Born in Virginia and gathering his first childhood memories in Atlanta, Georgia, he watched his mother nurse wounded Confederate soldiers and saw Union soldiers marching through Atlanta. The family later moved to Columbia, South Carolina, where the majority population were Black Americans, and then to Wilmington, North Carolina. He was a child of the Civil War and a Southerner of Reconstruction.

His father was a Presbyterian minister and a teacher at Columbia Theological Seminary and the Southwestern Presbyterian Theological University. He was a leader of the Presbyterian Church of the Confederate States of America, which leased out enslaved persons to organizations looking for help.

28th President of the United States

Getting a Formal Education

During Woodrow's formative years, public schools did not exist in the South, so he was mostly taught by his father. Although he occasionally attended makeshift schools set up by former Confederate soldiers. In 1873, he enrolled in a college outside Charlotte, North Carolina.

After a year, he transferred to the College of New Jersey (Princeton), from which he graduated in 1879. He later earned a Ph.D. in history and political science from Johns Hopkins University. He taught at various universities before landing a job as a professor of law and political economy at Princeton, at which he later became President of the university.

Whig Hall, College of New Jersey (Princeton)

Finding a Candidate to Control

Political bosses in New Jersey asked Professor Wilson to run for Governor assuming that, without any previous political experience, he would be easy to control. They were wrong.

He immediately wrote legislation that required primary candidates—the people who want to run for office—to be chosen by popular vote, rather than by party bosses. This was a popular movement among progressives of the day, and Wilson proved himself to be one of them. He also took a page from President Roosevelt and held press conferences. It all drew national attention, and he was soon running for President of the United States.

Charting a Path for Reform

No sooner did President Woodrow Wilson take the oath of office than he appeared before the first session of Congress to lay out his goals for reform. No President since John Adams had ever addressed Congress, and it signaled that things were going to be different. President Wilson was fully behind the progressive goals of improving the working life of ordinary citizens. He outlined his vision for lower tariffs, which worked against business monopolies, and signed it into law.

Woodrow Willson campaign poster for governor

President Wilson also settled the national banking system and monetary system debates that had consumed much of the previous century. The Legislature delivered to his desk the Federal Reserve Act of 1913, which set up twelve regional banks, with a government agency to oversee them. The system was given the authority to raise and lower interest rates, and to release additional currency, or coins and bills, into the economy if it deemed necessary.*

In response to many years of labor unrest, and numerous strikes, President Wilson created a Department of Labor and appointed a former Union leader to lead the new agency. He appointed the first Jewish lawyer to the Supreme Court, who had made his name fighting for women's rights and protecting children from unfair labor laws. He disappointed many Black Americans by not addressing civil rights issues, and in fact, he approved a new era of segregation throughout the federal government.

Entering World War I

As World War I broke out in Europe, President Wilson urged neutrality. Most Americans agreed with him. But when the Germans began a U-boat assault on American trading ships, Americans began to change their minds. The last straw was a letter written by Arthur Zimmerman, the German ambassador to Mexico, to the Mexican government.

In it, he tried to make a deal between Germany and Mexico. He explained that if Mexico would join Germany in the war, that Germany would help them retake New Mexico, Arizona, and Texas. Americans were furious, and President Wilson asked Congress to declare war on Germany.

Gearing Up for War

Now the country needed a method for gathering soldiers and getting them trained. So, Wilson signed the Selective Service Act in 1917, announcing that we were fighting to "make the world safe for democracy." At the time, the U.S. did not have a very big standing army. The new law made it legal to draft young men. Over the course of the

Woodrow Willson and his cabinet

war, about 2.8 million men were drafted, but that only represented about 72% of the army. The rest were volunteers.

To preserve energy and food for the army, Congress established Daylight Savings Time, which was supposed to cut back on citizens' use of electricity. Also, the newly created Food Administration urged Americans to have "Meatless Mondays" and to plant vegetable gardens.

Another law that President Wilson signed was controversial. It was the Espionage and Sedition Acts that made it illegal to criticize the government, or the war effort. Many Americans objected to the law, complaining that it was an unconstitutional limit on free speech. Under this law, the Post Office was opening people's mail, and neighbors were encouraged to turn each other in for criticizing the war effort.

The Presidential Footprint

At the end of the war, President Wilson tried to convince the United States to join the League of Nations. It was his vision for preventing future wars, to establish an organization meant to dissolve tensions and resolve arguments between nations before any war could start. Many European nations joined, and the League was set up. But the United States never joined it because joining implied that all the members agreed to defend each other, in case of future attacks. Many in Congress feared they would be giving up self-determination if they signed the pact.

Many historians, however, say that his establishment of the League of Nations set the U.S. on a path toward international leadership. In addition, Wilson's domestic reforms changed the Democratic Party, which had been run by political machine bosses, and transformed it into a reform party. He stood by the working man, and some say, softened the industrial age.

Many historians criticize him on this very point. For while he listened to the cries of the working man and supported his struggle, Wilson did not include Black Americans in these reforms. Nevertheless, many historians agree that in his influence on future generations, he ranks fifth behind Washington, Lincoln, Franklin Roosevelt, and Thomas Jefferson.

*For comprehension and vocabulary work, as well as a mini lesson on the Federal Reserve, see the *Discussion Guide*, pages 43-45.

Poster for Birth of a Nation, 1915

Birth: December 28, 1856   **Place:** Staunton, Virginia   **Occupation:** Professor, College Administrator, Public Official

Religion: Presbyterian   **Term of Office:** 1913 to 1921   **Death:** February 3, 1924

Position on Civil Rights and Immigration: President Wilson encouraged government agency directors to "reduce friction" in their departments. This was understood to mean segregate.

- During the Wilson years, applicants for government jobs were required to attach a photo to their applications.

- In 1915, President Wilson sponsored a private showing of *The Birth of a Nation.* The movie promoted the view that the Ku Klux Klan saved the South during the Reconstruction years.

Warren G. Harding

Chasing Popularity and Business Success

Warren Harding was one of six children born to parents who were both doctors. His mother earned her doctor's license based on her years of delivering babies and assisting her husband, who was a doctor.

With five siblings, young Warren experienced the rambunctious life of a boy on a farm and attended a one-room schoolhouse. At fourteen he enrolled in Ohio Central College and edited the school newspaper. He taught school for a while and then tried to be an insurance salesman before he and a few friends purchased the Marion Star newspaper. It was almost bankrupt, but they built it back to some success. He became known to local politicians through the Marion Star's unbiased reporting style.

29th President of the United States

Developing Friendships with Politicians

The newspaper, however, was more than just unbiased. Owing somewhat to Harding's friendly temperament, the paper never published an article that was critical of politicians.

He was also generous with his employees, sharing the profits with them and never firing anyone. He was so well-liked that he won two terms as Senator for the Ohio legislature, and one term as Lieutenant Governor before he went to Washington to serve in the Senate.

Running against the League of Nations

Warren Harding ran on the Republican ticket in 1920 as a candidate opposed to the League of Nations. But what was most important to the Republican party was that he had no political enemies. He was enormously popular, a quality that got him elected, but that proved a stumbling block in the presidency.

Since popularity was important to him, he appointed his friends to his cabinet, some of whom were dishonest, but all of whom liked to play poker and golf. As a result, his administration was uneven in talent and full of corruption. In one poker game, Harding gambled away an entire set of White House china. Moreover, several of his cabinet members went to jail for defrauding the government, and his Attorney General was impeached by Congress.

Supporting Some Changes

Yet, he did some good. He signed one bill to change the process for creating the federal budget—the Budget and Accounting Act of 1921. It allowed the President to create the budget, instead of individual government departments creating separate pieces of it.

He also spoke freely to support racial equality for Black Americans but did not support new laws to secure their civil rights. Yet, in support of freedom of speech, he asked the Justice Department to review the cases of each person who might have been unjustly arrested for protesting World War I. In that review, the Justice Department pardoned and released the American Socialist leader, Eugene Debs, who had once campaigned for President. In a show of support, President Harding invited him to the White House for a meeting.

Spreading Good Will

With his corrupt friends all around him, he worried about the level of scandal that was erupting. So he traveled to the West, planning to spread some goodwill by meeting people and shaking hands. But during that trip, he suffered a heart attack and died. He could not stop the shame of his cabinet's corruption from hitting the newspapers and swamping his legacy.*

The Presidential Footprint

Some historians point out that Warren G. Harding suffered in comparison to Woodrow Wilson who had a vision for what the presidency could be. Yet President Harding is criticized for not having any vision at all for the country, nor a strong sense of morality. He saw the presidency as a ceremonial position. Though he gets some credit for having spoken out in support of racial equality, and for releasing Eugene Debs from prison, he is often ranked as one of our worst presidents.

*For comprehension and vocabulary work, see the *Discussion Guide*, page 46.

Birth: November 2, 1865   **Place:** Corsica, Ohio   **Occupation:** Editor, Publisher

Religion: Baptist   **Term of Office:** 1921 to 1923   **Death:** August 2, 1923

Position on Civil Rights and Immigration: President Harding addressed the University of Alabama on the evils of segregation and the importance of racial equality.

- He signed the Johnson Immigrant Quota Act of 1921 which severely restricted the number of immigrants to only 3% of the number currently living in the U.S.

- He supported the Dyer Anti-Lynching Bill which passed in the House but was killed by Southern Democrats in the Senate.

- He supported women's rights, as his mother was a midwife and doctor.

Calvin Coolidge

Inheriting Puritan Values

President Calvin Coolidge took pride in being a hard-working New Englander of old Puritan stock. His family had settled in Massachusetts 150 years earlier, and then moved to Vermont. His father was a successful farmer, postmaster, and general store owner. Young Cal worked hard alongside his father, filling the woodbin, bringing in hay, and storing grain.

He also worked hard at school, and though he was not brilliant, he studied hard. He excelled at rhetoric and oratory, winning awards for his speeches. Notably in college, he won first place for an essay called "The Principles Fought for in the American Revolution" in a contest sponsored by the National Society of the Sons of the American Revolution.

30th President of the United States

Serving the Public

Calvin Coolidge followed in his father's footsteps and became active in local politics. He rose steadily on the political ladder and was dedicated to his fellow citizens. He started as a local Northampton City Councilman, then was elected Mayor of Northampton. He later served in the state Senate as President of the Senate before being elected Lieutenant Governor and finally Governor of Massachusetts.

He drew national attention when he called the National Guard to end a strike by the Boston police. He sternly told the leader of the American Federation of Labor that "There is no right to strike against the public safety by anybody, anywhere, anytime." His decision made national headlines.

Although later historians now see it as a very conservative action, overall, Governor Coolidge enacted many progressive changes during his term. Owing to his new national profile, Calvin Coolidge went to the Republican National Convention hoping to win the ticket for President. Instead, he was Vice President on the Warren G. Harding ticket.

Turning Down the National Temperature

When Harding passed away, Coolidge was vacationing at his family's home in Plymouth Notch, Vermont. He received the news, knelt in prayer, and then went downstairs at 2:24 a.m. His father was present, and since he was a justice of the peace, he administered the oath of office to his son. As a testament to his later campaign slogan, "Keep Cool with Coolidge," he took the oath and went back to bed.

President Coolidge was a welcome change for the country. As he took office, the manifold corruptions of the Harding administration were exploding in the press. Coolidge's first acts were to fire most of Harding's old friends.

As the Coolidge administration got underway, it was clear that he did not believe the presidency was a platform for political action. This was partly a reaction against the bold activism of Roosevelt and Wilson. Yet Coolidge did hold regular press conferences and spoke on the radio one to two times per month.

Landing on the Side of States' Rights

He believed that most difficulties should be resolved by the states, yet he believed in running a tight federal ship with a balanced budget. He is most remembered for two economic issues: signing the Revenue Acts of 1924 and 1926, which cut taxes for the wealthy. Americans saw these actions as pivotal support for the luxury living of the Jazz Age.

However, his lack of attention to the depressed farm market is often pointed to as a potential cause of the Great Depression. During World War I, farmers stepped up production to feed Americans, the army, and Europeans whose farmlands were bombed-out wastelands. Farmers struggled to regain their prosperity as the enlarged need for their crops disappeared after the war. Twice, Congress stepped in, passing legislation that would have subsidized the farmers, but President Coolidge vetoed them both. When the Great Depression hit, nearly five thousand rural banks closed, and hundreds of farmers lost their lands.*

The Presidential Footprint

While Calvin Coolidge was popular for his honesty and wit, most historians did not think he was a good president. They acknowledge that his temperament was a welcome change from the corrupt Harding presidency, yet Coolidge had a sense of humility that did not suit the job. When farmers' economic problems came across his desk, he did not think it was his job to work with Congress to develop solutions. In fact, when the Great Depression hit, the failure of rural banks was one of the major problems of the period.

*For comprehension and vocabulary work, see the *Discussion Guide*, page 47.

Birth: July 4, 1872   **Place:** Plymouth Notch, Vermont   **Occupation:** Lawyer

Religion: Congregationalist   **Term of Office:** 1923 to 1929   **Death:** January 5, 1933

Position on Civil Rights and Immigration: President Coolidge prompted Congress to budget $500,000 to Howard University, a historically Black college, for a medical school.

- In thanks to American Indian veterans of World War I, Coolidge signed the Indian Citizenship Act, though they were not given voting rights.

- He approved a memorial commemorating the "Negro's contributions to the achievements of America."

- Coolidge defended a black man who was running for Congress. *The Chicago Defender*, a black newspaper, praised his support with this headline: "Cal Coolidge Tells Kluxers When to Stop."

Herbert Hoover

Pulling Ahead of Misfortune

Young Herbert lost his father when he was six years old. His dad was a blacksmith and sold farm equipment before he died suddenly of a heart attack. Then only three years later, Herbert's mother died of pneumonia. He and his older brother and little sister were passed among relatives before they settled with an uncle in Oregon.

Herbert was shy and fearful, but he pulled ahead of his misfortune, earning average grades in school. Despite lackluster performance, he enrolled in Stanford University, majoring in geology, and working his way through school as a clerk in the administration building. He showed creative business skills and earned money setting up a laundry service for students.

31st President of the United States

Building His Reputation

After graduating, he worked for a mining company, inspecting mines and reporting back about their suitability for purchase, traveling through Australia and China until 1902. During a rebellion in China, his wife nursed injured Westerners, and Herbert fought to defend a city near the uprising. Later, he opened his own mining consulting business and traveled the world. He was already well-known in his field when World War I broke out while he was in London.

He earned international thanks by organizing emergency relief for Belgium, which had lost its food supply when Germany invaded. He shipped millions of pounds of food and did the same for 20 million starving Russians who were suffering from their own internal revolution.

In thanks, President Wilson appointed him Director of the U.S. Food Administration during World War I and as a diplomat for the peace conference after the war. Moreover, President Harding appointed him Secretary of Commerce, a position he kept under President Coolidge.

Moving into the Presidency

On March 4, 1929 he entered the White House carrying the promise he had made to Americans to start a "New Day." His first task was to help the farmers.

While others had grown wealthy during the 1920s, farmers' incomes had been shrinking. President Hoover believed firmly that a Federal Farm Board, supplied with $500 million, would help farm cooperatives manage crop production and get crops to market quickly. But the farmers wanted payments from the government. He argued with Congress over the right solution, and they finally set up the Federal Farm Board.

Facing the Stock Market Crash

But by October 29 of that year, the stock market crashed, and Americans did indeed enter a "new day," though it was not what they had hoped for. President Hoover's initial response was to encourage people to help each other. He also tried to avoid setting up massive government relief efforts. He thought that if Americans volunteered, they would get through this temporary crisis. It turned out that as a business manager, he was outstanding, but as a politician, he did not have enough understanding of government processes to lead Congress to pass effective legislation.

He called for local governments to expand public works projects to employ their residents. Nothing seemed to be helping. By 1931, two years into President Hoover's term, he believed that the worst of the Depression was over. This was not a result of incompetence on his part. Many economists believed the same. But by June of that year, statistics showed that more than eight million people were still out of work, with no end in sight. Bank failures were increasing. Social workers in the thick of the volunteer army reported little progress. Americans were beginning to turn to other candidates for a president who could help.*

The Presidential Footprint

Lately, historians are more forgiving of President Hoover. Although none of his ideas relieved Depression suffering, many now think that nothing would have stopped the downward economic spiral. Yet, they also think that Hoover deserves credit for turning to sociologists of the day who were gathering statistics about different social groups, information that was helpful far into the future. Despite these good efforts, most historians think that Hoover was as poor a politician, as he was a great humanitarian. He may have had his best years before he became president.

*For comprehension and vocabulary work, see the *Discussion Guide*, page 48.

Birth: August 10, 1874 **Place:** West Branch, Iowa **Occupation:** Engineer

Religion: Quaker **Term of Office:** 1929 to 1933 **Death:** October 20, 1964

Position on Civil Rights and Immigration: When Illinois sent the first Black Representative to Congress since Reconstruction, First Lady Hoover invited his wife to the White House, ignoring criticism for her actions.

- When Hoover was Secretary of Commerce, he desegrated two of the offices. Complaints from white congressmen were so fierce that black members of the National Association for the Advancement of Colored People (NAACP) thought they should join the Democratic party.

- He instructed the Department of the Interior to attend to the poverty-stricken Native Americans.

The Great Depression

This photo was sent to President Roosevelt with the following note enclosed. "Rolla Kansas, May 6-35. Mr. Franklin D. Roosevelt. Washington DC. Dear Mr. Roosevelt, we are mailing you a picture of the dust storm which came April 14-35. This was a northeast wind and darkness came. When this hit us the sun was shining bright and darkness was coming on at 3 o'clock in the evening. Taken from the water tower one hundred feet high. Yours, truly, Chas. P. Williams. Rolla Kansas."

Social Security was established during the Great Depression to help the elderly when they retire. It was one of the many programs that Congress started to help Americans climb out of the poverty they had fallen into.

The Farm Security Administration reported: "Erosion—Cotton was grown on this field twenty-five years ago. Chilton County, Alabama."

The original caption for this photo read: "Police and strikers battle in San Francisco's 1934 general strike. See pg 167 of the Desperate Years, by Horan. San Francisco, Cailfornia."

In the early years of the depression, thousands of people ran to banks to withdraw all their money. Here, a crowd gathers outside a bank in 1933.

Franklin Delano Roosevelt

Growing Up in Luxury

Franklin Roosevelt was an only child, whose mother was from a wealthy family, and whose father was a successful businessman. Franklin grew up on a large estate north of New York City that hired dozens of farm workers and household staff. Though other children his own age were few, his mother was a very attentive parent. Franklin learned to read and write at home, but then attended Groton School, a private school for wealthy and influential citizens.

32nd President of the United States

It was at this stage that Franklin became aware of his very famous, though distant cousin, Theodore Roosevelt, whom he grew to admire. At age 18, Franklin enrolled in Harvard and became engrossed in numerous extra-curricular activities. Though he was gaining much-needed socialization skills, his academic work suffered. He graduated in 1903 and then returned for one year of graduate work, becoming editor of the famed student newspaper, The Crimson. It was during his college years that he declared himself a Democrat, despite his famous cousin's Republican affiliation.

Meeting Eleanor

At a New Year's reception sponsored by Theodore Roosevelt in the White House, Franklin met his fifth cousin, Eleanor, who was the President's niece. They later married, with Uncle Teddy giving the bride away, since her father, Teddy's younger brother, had died when she was 10. Franklin and Eleanor had five children.

Stepping Into the Political World

As with his elder cousin, Franklin had a keen interest in public service, and he won a state senate seat on his first campaign. He ran as a reform candidate and early on worked on behalf of farmers, against the political machine in New York City. Despite the Democratic political machine's distrust for him, he won his re-election campaign.

Shortly into his term, the Secretary of the Navy under Woodrow Wilson appointed him assistant secretary. He was thrilled to follow in Teddy's footsteps, who had also held that job, and was interested in increasing the Navy's size and capabilities.

Though his political career was off to a good start,

Young Franklin on a horse

in a run for the U.S. Senate seat from New York in 1914, he lost. Furthermore, although he lost again as Vice President on the 1920s losing Democratic ticket, he was gaining a national reputation.

Fighting against Life-Threatening Illness

It was all threatened in 1921, when Roosevelt was stricken with polio, a dangerous and deadly infection of the spinal cord. Eleanor proved to be a staunch support during this period as he fought for his health, eventually regaining some mobility, though he was in a wheelchair for the rest of his life. So that he could stay in politics, Eleanor became an active partner in the Democratic party for him, becoming his mobile collaborator.

Franklin D. Roosevelt at the Groton School

During the rest of the 1920's Franklin continually suppressed rumors about his illness. Eventually, he won the Governorship of New York by a slim margin and re-election in 1930. The Great Depression had just begun.

Restoring Public Trust in Banking

When FDR, as he came to be called, took the oath of office in 1933, Americans had been suffering through the Great Depression for about three years. They participated in numerous "runs" on banks, in which hundreds ran to the bank and withdrew all their money. People feared that the bank would close, just as thousands of banks had already done. At least 25% of all Americans had lost their jobs. Starvation was a very real threat.

FDR's first order of business was to restore public trust in the banking system. He ordered all the banks to temporarily close. Then he called a special session of Congress, during which they quickly passed his proposal. A committee would review every bank that had closed and create three categories:

Banks closed by the thousands in the early years of the Great Depression. Here, a crowd gathers to withdraw all their money.

1. Banks that could be saved with some help;

2. Banks that could re-open without any government help;

3. Banks that should close forever.

But he didn't forget about the American people. Only eight days after he took office and had the plan in place, he went on the radio to "chat" with Americans and explain the plan. As many historians have noted, FDR had a particularly appropriate personality for this type of problem. He was optimistic, unafraid, flexible, and practical. In his radio "Fireside Chats," he calmed Americans' fears and gave them hope for the future. He demonstrated what he had promised in his inaugural address: "The only thing we have to fear is fear itself." It worked. As American banks began to slowly re-open, people went back and re-deposited almost 1$ billion dollars.

Restoring Hope

FDR had set the tone for the rest of his presidency. He regularly spoke to Americans in "Fireside Chats." He was proactive in developing plans to jump-start the economy. Despite previous presidents who did not think it was the government's job to help

Roosevelt giving a fireside chat

people, President Franklin Delano Roosevelt used the government to create jobs programs, and to stabilize the financial system.

Throughout the 1930s, the Depression continued. FDR created jobs like the Civilian Conservation Corps, working in the National Parks building paths, picnic areas, pavilions, and drinking fountains, most of which Americans still enjoy today. He created financial agencies that provided structure to the banking industry. Still in use today, Americans get housing loans from the Federal Housing Authority, and the Federal National Mortgage Association. He set up relief programs for farmers, and work programs to bring electricity to rural areas.

Not every program was a success. In the early years of the Depression, Congress set up the National Recovery Administration. Its goal was to help businesses regulate themselves. It did not completely work, since committees from big businesses wrote the ethical codes for its processes. Even though the government required them to allow unions to operate, small businesses complained, and in the end, even businesses who signed up to obey the rules only did so when it suited them. Ultimately, the organization dissolved.

Hanging on to Neutrality

Throughout the 1930s, as FDR continued to tackle the financial problems plaguing the country, war was brewing in Europe. By 1939, World War II had started, but Americans refused to get involved in Europe's problems. In just four years, Congress passed five laws defining America's official neutrality. FDR had won re-election in 1936 and was in his second term.

Roosevelt giving a speech in 1931

As FDR monitored the growing threat in Europe and Asia, he tried to prepare Americans to relax their neutrality, but they were not budging. On two occasions, he convinced Congress to adjust the neutrality laws by allowing our Allies to buy arms from us. Then, inching closer to involvement, he won passage of the Lend-Lease Act, which lent Great Britain and France ships and airplanes in return for allowing the U.S. the use of military bases in their countries. It was a way to set up American bases in the Allied territory without joining the war just yet. He won election to a third term in 1940.

Inching Closer to Involvement

FDR and England's Prime Minister, Winston Churchill, had been talking throughout the early days of the war, developing a vision for a post-war world. FDR had slowly chipped away at America's penchant for isolationism. When the Nazis began to attack Great Britain by air, and then by sea, FDR told Americans that we would provide them all aid necessary, though "short of war." This vague declaration rattled the isolationists.

Entering World War II

On December 7, 1941, the Japanese attacked the American fleet anchored in Pearl Harbor, Hawaii. It was a surprise attack in the early morning hours, and over 2,000 sailors were killed. Now, FDR asked Congress for a declaration of war. In FDR and Churchill's earlier meetings, FDR developed his vision, like Woodrow Wilson's, for a United Nations organization that would be a watchdog to help prevent future wars. But that was four years away. There was still a war to win, and the U.S. was committed to fight in both the Pacific Ocean, North Africa, and in Europe.

While the military leaders armed, trained, and transported soldiers and munitions, they also planned how to carry out individual battles. But the larger, international goals were developed by FDR, Winston Churchill, and Joseph Stalin, the leader of the Soviet Union. Stalin was eager for the U.S. and Great Britain to invade Europe from the north, thus relieving the stress on his troops, who were fighting in eastern Europe.

Roosevelt and Churchill met before the U.S. entered the war, on a ship in the Atlantic, to make post-war plans.

Making Plans to Invade Europe

These issues were discussed at a conference of the three leaders in the city of Casablanca, Morocco, in North Africa. But FDR, advised by his military leaders, wanted American troops to gain some experience before invading northern Europe. Winston Churchill urged an invasion of southern Europe through Italy. FDR agreed, and together Churchill and FDR promised Stalin that they would invade northern Europe the following spring.

By November of 1943, the three met again in Tehran, Iran to plan the next phase of the war. Churchill and FDR promised Stalin that they would finally invade northern Europe. They were planning the great D-Day invasion of France, which they had hoped would bring about the final phase of the war. After the success of the D-Day invasion in 1944, the leaders met one last time at Yalta, in Crimea on the Black Sea. FDR was visibly ill. He was suffering from a heart condition, and the difficulty of leading the nation through the Great Depression and then World War II was becoming too much for him.

Roosevelt reviewing troops in Morocco

Crossing the German Border

Shortly after the meeting in Yalta, Great Britain, France, and the United States troops crossed the western German borders. The Soviet Union breached the German borders on the East. The end of the war seemed at hand. Although Americans worried about FDR's health, he managed in the last few months of the war to deliver a few rousing speeches that allayed concerns. Yet, his doctors and family knew the truth. He won his last re-election to the presidency in 1944. In April of 1945, he died, just a few months before the end of the war. It ended on May 7 in Europe and on August 14 in the Pacific.*

The Presidential Footprint

It is not possible to state briefly what FDR did for the United States, given that his impact was powerful and farsighted. Although many of his efforts to resolve the Great Depression were criticized and others failed, many other of his programs are still in effect today. Under FDR's leadership, the presidency itself changed from being not only the leader of the Executive branch of government, but into a dynamic inspiration and visionary of legislation as well. In that regard, he stood on the shoulders of both Theodore Roosevelt and Woodrow Wilson. Though he surpassed them both.

*For comprehension and vocabulary work, as well as a mini lesson on the Great Depression, see the *Discussion Guide*, pages 49-51.

Birth: January 30, 1882   **Place:** Hyde Park, New York   **Occupation:** Public Official, Lawyer

Religion: Episcopalian   **Term of Office:** 1933 to 1945   **Death:** April 12, 1945

Position on Civil Rights and Immigration: FDR, partly from the influence of his wife Eleanor, hired several Black American advisors into the government. They were known as his "Black cabinet."

- Because of the Depression, he claimed he could not afford to lose the votes of Southern Democrats in Congress. Therefore, he never pushed the passage of an anti-lynching bill.

- FDR signed an executive order which set up a Fair Employment Practices Commission.

Harry S. Truman

Dealing with Poor Eyesight

Harry S. Truman was born on a farm in rural Independence, Missouri outside of Kansas City. The town hosted droves of wagon trains heading West to pick up the Oregon Trail. Despite the promise of adventure he witnessed, his mother discouraged him from rough play. She feared for him, as he had poor eyesight and was not a robust boy.

Quitting School

The family suffered through the farming troubles of the early twentieth century, and after high school, Harry had to quit the business school he attended to get work. Besides farming, he worked in a bank, for the Kansas City Star newspaper in their mailroom, and for

33rd President of the United States

a construction company. In 1914, just as World War I was starting in Europe, Harry's dad died. Although it was a difficult time for him, he was finally able to leave the farm and strike out on his own.

He had never been able to enlist in the military due to his poor eyesight. So in 1917, after a few years of owning a mining business, Harry joined the local National Guard, which was later renamed the 129th Artillery Regiment.

Developing Leadership Skills

Finally, young Harry found a job that he liked, and his fellow soldiers liked him too. They respected his leadership, and he rose quickly to Captain, taking a regiment that had a bad reputation and turning them into a crack fighting unit. They deployed to Europe and fought in a battle east of Paris, near the German border, and in the Argonnes campaign, one of the last battles of the war.

Returning home, he opened a men's clothing shop with an army buddy. As with most businesses in the early 1920s, it was successful for a short while. When the recession of 1921 hit, however, he went out of business. But he had become popular and gained the attention of the Kansas City Democratic political machine. They tapped him to run for local office, in which he managed the building of roads and other infrastructure.

By 1934, he won an election to the U.S. Senate. He was a strong supporter of FDR's New Deal policies and worked hard sponsoring bills to improve the country's laws for transportation industries. He also led an investigation into wasteful defense spending. By 1944, FDR chose him to be Vice President.

Accepting an Unexpected Call to Service

Truman was only Vice President for a few months before FDR died. About one month after he took office, Hitler died, and Germany surrendered. But war in the Pacific was still ongoing. Military leaders were training men for an invasion of the Japanese mainland. Experts estimated that the war with Japan would last another year, with as many as 200,000 more American casualties.

At the last conference of the war, President Truman met with Stalin of the Soviet Union, and the new Prime Minister of Great Britain, in Potsdam, Germany. While there, Truman received top-secret news that the test of the atom bomb had been successful. From the conference, Truman approved an ultimatum to the Japanese Emperor demanding their surrender, though no response was received.

So, President Truman ordered the military to drop the atomic bomb. The first bomb dropped on Hiroshima, Japan on the morning of August 6, 1945. Without a response from the Japanese government, the U.S. military dropped a second bomb on Nagasaki the morning of August 9. The Japanese Emperor surrendered on August 14. World War II was over.*

The Presidential Footprint

Historians' opinions about President Harry S. Truman have changed over the years. When he left office, he was very unpopular. But it did not take long for Americans to change their minds about him. They began to see him as a Midwestern everyman, who was not like the professional politicians in Washington. Historians began to appreciate the difficulties he was faced with in the aftermath of World War II. Moreover, some historians say Truman was the first true "civil rights" president of the twentieth century.

*For comprehension and vocabulary work, see the *Discussion Guide*, page 52.

Birth: May 8, 1884   **Place:** Lamar, Missouri   **Occupation:** Farmer, Businessman, Public Official

Religion: Baptist   **Term of Office:** 1945 to 1953   **Death:** December 26, 1972

Position on Civil Rights and Immigration: In 1948, President Truman addressed Congress with a bold speech, urging them to develop civil rights legislation with protection from lynching for Black Americans.

- Because of strong Southern Democratic opposition, Congress did nothing. So, Truman signed Executive Order 9981 desegregating the military, and banning discrimination in the federal government.

- In 1947, Truman addressed 10,000 members of the National Association for the Advancement of Colored People (NAACP), affirming his belief that it was the federal government's job to secure the civil rights of all Americans.

Dwight D. Eisenhower

Overcoming Institutional Opinions

Although Dwight Eisenhower was born in Dennison, Texas, the family moved to Abilene, Kansas where his father got a job as a mechanic in a local creamery. Young David played football and went hunting and fishing. He showed no special interest in school and spent his time reading military history. At age 21, he earned an appointment to West Point where he was an average student who relaxed with his friends. None of his teachers thought he would make a good officer.

His first assignments were unremarkable. But while he was at Camp Meade in Maryland, he published an article explaining his idea that the military could make better use of tanks. His commanding officer scolded him, saying that Eisenhower did not have enough experience to criticize his elders.

34th President of the United States

Finally, he was transferred to the Panama Canal Zone under a commanding officer who appreciated his ideas. He sent Eisenhower to the prestigious Command and General Staff College in Fort Leavenworth, Kansas. From there, Eisenhower began to move up in his career until he became the Supreme Commander of Operation Overlord, the codename for the D-Day invasion of France in World War II.

Taking the Oath and Fighting the Cold War

The World War II victory made General Eisenhower a national hero, and he successfully ran for President in 1953. While the end-of-war euphoria manifested in young families filling up the suburbs, the country was nevertheless still facing serious difficulties overseas. Although the Soviet Union had been our ally during the war, they quickly broke their promises about post-war Europe. They took over East Germany and refused to let them have free elections.

Eisenhower also inherited a tense relationship with China because they supported North Korea in the Korean War. The tension between the U.S., the Soviet Union, and China became known as the Cold War.

As a military man, President Eisenhower convincingly used threats of nuclear weapons. Once in a tense conversation about China, he said that he would not hesitate to use a nuclear weapon, "exactly as you would use a bullet." It was a veiled threat to get China to the negotiating table. All three world powers used threats like these during the Cold War while they built up their stockpile of weapons.

Growing Fear of Communism

At home, American fear of communism grew, especially as Senator McCarthy from Wisconsin accused people in the government, Hollywood, and the military of being spies. During the atomic bomb project, there had been many active spies, so Eisenhower had reason to be watchful. Yet Senator McCarthy never presented any evidence, and the country's fear increased.

Many people thought Senator McCarthy was going too far, and that President Eisenhower was being too quiet. Yet, he did not want to publicly criticize McCarthy since it would likely only lead to a senseless argument. However, Eisenhower had been the first president to use television to his advantage with commercials in his campaign, and cameras at his press conferences. When one of McCarthy's hearings was televised, Eisenhower did not stop him. Americans could finally see his venomous behavior, and they turned against him.

Another aspect of the Cold War was the proxy war in Vietnam, in which the United States supported South Vietnam's fight against communism.*

Developing the Interstate Highway System

President Eisenhower also approved the development of the interstate highways. They served to connect far flung points in the country, bringing Americans into the modern era. But they also served to erode the cities, as people began to move out to the suburbs and drive in for work.

The Presidential Footprint

When President Eisenhower left office, many Americans thought of him as a "do-nothing" President. But over the decades, many historians have studied his papers and now argue that he was quite active behind the scenes. While this can be an important strategy, some historians criticize him for not visibly confronting Senator McCarthy. They assert that the President should have known when to come to the foreground. Yet, he is regarded more highly now than when he first left office.

*For comprehension and vocabulary work, as well as a mini lesson on the Vietnam War, see the *Discussion Guide*, pages 53 and 55.

Birth: October 14, 1890   **Place:** Dennison, Texas   **Occupation:** Soldier

Religion: Presbyterian   **Term of Office:** 1953 to 1961   **Death:** March 28, 1969

Position on Civil Rights and Immigration: President Eisenhower finished the desegregation of the military and federal government, begun by President Truman.

- He appointed Chief Justice Warren to the Supreme Court, who wrote the famous opinion that segregated schools were unconstitutional, in *Brown v. Board of Education.*

- He signed the first civil rights bill in over eighty years, although the bill he submitted to Congress had been severely weakened when it came back across his desk.

John F. Kennedy

Growing Up Privileged

John Fitzgerald Kennedy was born into a privileged life in a wealthy suburb of Boston. His grandfather had been mayor of Boston, and young John's childhood was filled with sailboats, private schools, and summer homes. His only challenge was chronic illness, including a bout with scarlet fever. When he enrolled in Harvard, he said that his only knowledge of the Great Depression was what he read in history books.

In 1938, his father was appointed Ambassador to Great Britain, and he went with him to London, finishing his course work from abroad. While there, he wrote his senior essay called "Why England Slept," discussing England's lack of preparedness for World War II. It became a bestseller.

35th President of the United States

Serving His Country

At the outbreak of America's involvement in World War II, he tried to enlist but was rejected because of poor health. However, his father invoked his connections, and John was accepted into the Navy.

As a young lieutenant, he was given command of a small torpedo-scouting boat. One night, the crew was sleeping and had not posted a watch—against regulations. A Japanese destroyer rammed them, and Lt. Kennedy guided all his crew on a three-mile swim to the nearest island. Although the Navy found negligence in the lack of a posted watch, they still awarded him a medal for getting his crew to safety.

Polishing His Image and Winning

After the war, Kennedy worked as a journalist before winning a seat in the U.S. House of Representatives. He served three terms representing a Boston working-class neighborhood. In 1952, he ran for the U.S. Senate, defeating a Republican from another well-established political family.

Perhaps because he desired a political career, he kept his poor health a secret. He was weak from malaria, contracted during the war. He also had a condition called Addison's disease, which prevented his body from producing certain hormones. Despite all this, his political campaigns always portrayed him as young and healthy.

Gaining National Name Recognition

Although he often took time out to convalesce, he was re-elected to the Senate in 1958 and was assigned to the Foreign Relations Committee. From that position, he gained a national profile, criticizing President Eisenhower's foreign policy. With national name recognition, he proceeded into the 1960 campaign for president.

He won with promises to look to the future with a new American generation, staffing up with young intellectuals and challenging the country to explore a New Frontier: "Ask not what your country can do for you, but what you can do for your country." As early as 1961, President Kennedy challenged the country to set foot on the moon by the end of the decade, in response to the Soviet Union's success in launching the first spaceship to orbit Earth. Americans had been shocked that we seemed to be losing the technology race, a major feature of the Cold War.

Another aspect of the Cold War was the proxy war in Vietnam, in which the United States supported South Vietnam's fight against communism.*

Supporting the Civil Rights Movement

When JFK became president, it was partly through the support of Black American voters of the new civil rights movement. In 1955, Rosa Parks refused to give her seat to a white woman on a bus in Montgomery, Alabama. It gave new energy to Black Americans' efforts to claim their civil rights, and Martin Luther King became its most recognizable leader.

Yet, Kennedy's reluctance to push a civil rights bill through Congress disappointed these voters. He had been concerned that Southern Democrats would defeat the bill, and he had decided to wait until his second term to attempt it. So it wasn't until late in 1963 that he finally submitted a civil rights bill to Congress. It would be up to his successor to get it passed and signed into law.

Death and the Presidential Footprint

On November 22, 1963, President Kennedy was shot and killed while riding in a convertible during a parade in Dallas, Texas. Because his presidency was cut short, many historians feel uncertain about his legacy. He did not live to see Americans land on the moon, nor the passage of the civil rights act.

*For comprehension and vocabulary work, see the *Discussion Guide*, page 54.

Birth: May 29, 1917   **Place:** Brookline, Massachusetts   **Occupation:** Author, U.S. Navy Officer, Journalist, Public Official

Religion: Roman Catholic   **Term of Office:** 1961 to 1963   **Death:** November 22, 1963

Position on Civil Rights and Immigration: During the presidential campaign, civil rights leader Martin Luther King was arrested in Atlanta. Presidential candidate JFK phoned his wife expressing concern for MLK's safety. JFK's brother, attorney Robert Kennedy worked with a judge to get MLK released.

- President Kennedy appointed Black Americans to high-level jobs in his administration. His attorney general, Robert Kennedy, initiated lawsuits in support of voting rights.

- JFK appointed the Vice President to chair the President's Committee on Equal Employment Opportunity.

Lyndon B. Johnson

Acceding under Shocking Conditions

On November 22, 1963, Vice President Johnson was riding in the motorcade two cars behind President and Mrs. Kennedy. In the frenzied aftermath of the shots that rang out, the Vice President's car rushed to the hospital. As soon as he arrived, there was no waiting for the news. President Kennedy had already died.

The Vice President was flown back to Washington, D.C. on Air Force One, but not before the Honorable Sarah T. Hughes, federal district judge of northern Texas, administered the oath of office. Although Lyndon B. Johnson had always been an ambitious politician, the circumstances of his promotion were not an occasion for celebration.

36th President of the United States

Rising above Physical Circumstances

Lyndon Johnson was the eldest of five children born to Sam and Rebekah Johnson. They were a Texan family whose ancestors had been among the earliest European settlers to the region and had fought for the Confederacy. Lyndon grew up in a house that had no electricity or running water, but he aspired to more than his surroundings indicated. He attended a one-room schoolhouse in rural Texas and graduated with a high school class of six students.

He had not been a particularly good student, and it took him two attempts before he was admitted to the Southwest Texas State Teachers College. He became a teacher and was assigned to a low-income, rural school, not unlike the one he himself had attended. He was devoted to his students and encouraged them to reach beyond their current circumstances.

Going Out on the Political Road

During his early teaching days, he volunteered in some local political campaigns and became an aid to a Congressman in Washington. He loved the work and swiftly rose to his own elected seat, representing his home district in Washington at only twenty-eight years old. Working harder than most other junior congressmen, he even managed to get funding for his home district to install electricity.

During World War II, his congressional contacts helped him get an officer's commission. In that job, he became the congressional inspector of the war's progress in the Pacific. He was still in Congress, but his work focused on the war effort.

Shortly after World War II, he was elected Senator for Texas. He gained national attention, as he quickly became one of the most powerful Senators in the country. His influence was felt by other southern Senators who succumbed to Johnson's persuasion and voted for the watered-down Civil Rights Act of 1957. By 1960, he was Vice President on the Kennedy ticket.

Evolving JFK's Vision into Johnson's Great Society

President Johnson took President Kennedy's optimism about a "New Frontier" and expanded it to include his vision of a "Great Society." It included the fulfillment of the promise of civil rights for Black Americans and other underserved members of society. Johnson's sweeping legislative victories included conservation laws, support for Americans as consumers, protection for voting rights, revisions to immigration laws, and funding to support the arts and humanities.

He shepherded the fulfillment of Kennedy's dream to land Americans on the moon. For him, the Great Society was characterized by well-funded education and a new Department of Housing and Urban Development. He also specifically announced a "war on poverty." This involved special agencies set up in cities across the country whose job was to funnel federal funds to the right programs, meant to support education, mental health services, job training, and other activities to give the impoverished hope. One of these programs was called Head Start and is still running today.*

The Presidential Footprint

Although President Lyndon B. Johnson had great vision for Americans, the amount of funding spent on these programs often created divisiveness. Many were concerned about the growing size of the government, while others criticized the programs' effectiveness. Johnson's legacy is also tarnished by the difficulties of the seemingly endless Vietnam War, which was another aspect of the Cold War. The war ran directly counter to the concept of a "Great Society." Many historians today still evaluate Johnson's presidency as one of deep contradictions.

*For comprehension and vocabulary work, see the *Discussion Guide*, page 56.

Birth: August 27, 1908   **Place:** Johnson City, Texas   **Occupation:** Teacher, Public Official
Religion: Disciples of Christ   **Term of Office:** 1963 to 1969   **Death:** January 22, 1973

Position on Civil Rights and Immigration: Appointed Thurgood Marshall to the Supreme Court and Robert Weaver as Secretary of Housing and Urban Development, both the first Black Americans to serve in those high-level positions.

- Signed the Civil Rights Act of 1964 and the Voting Rights Act of 1965.

- Appointed more black judges to the court system than any previous President.

Richard M. Nixon

Overcoming Grief

Richard M. Nixon was the second of five sons born in a small southern California town. His parents were Frank and Hannah, devoted members of their local Quaker church. Frank Nixon owned a ranch that was not profitable, so he sold it and moved to Whittier. There, he owned a gas station and a grocery store. They were a religious, hard-working family visited by tragedy. Richard's brother Harold died at age 23 of tuberculosis. Another brother died when he was only 7 years old of a brain disease.

Finding a Way to Serve His Country

Richard did very well in school and won a scholarship to attend the Law School at Duke University. He graduated in 1937, four

37th President of the United States

years before the U.S. joined World War II. As a Quaker, he was eligible to apply for conscientious objector status, or someone who objects to war on religious grounds and therefore asks not to fight. But he enlisted in the Navy in 1942 and served as a naval control officer in the South Pacific. He did not see any combat, but he served well and resigned as a Lieutenant Commander after the war ended.

When Nixon ran his first campaign for the U.S. House of Representatives, he used tactics that have since been called "smear campaigns." He used a campaign style that did not focus on the issues. Instead, Nixon only advertised suspicious things about his opponent. Although it's a less desirable way to campaign, he won the election and went to Washington as a Representative from California.

He was assigned to the House Un-American Committee on which he investigated government employees who were suspected of being Communist spies. During the late 1940s and through the 1950s, Americans were very afraid of communist infiltration. While there had been some well-publicized spy cases, most of the people the committee focused on were not spies. Their work ultimately became known as a giant smear campaign led by the Chairman, Senator Joseph McCarthy.

In 1952, Richard Nixon ran as Vice President on General Eisenhower's ticket. Working with the Eisenhower administration gave him a great deal of foreign policy experience, traveling to many Asian countries, as well as throughout Latin America and Africa.

President Richard M. Nixon

In 1968, Richard Nixon became the thirty-seventh President of the United States. Even though as a Senator, he had made his name by searching for communists in the government, when he became President, he was determined to improve U.S. relationships with China, a large communist country. One of the first things he did was to respectfully call them the People's Republic of China. Then through a combination of opportunity, planning, and media blitz, the United States ping pong team was invited to Beijing, China. President Nixon followed up with a visit of his own. America was captivated to see the interior of a country that had not allowed visitors for many decades.

As with four previous presidents, he made secretive decisions about Vietnam and lied to the American people about them. But in 1973, he ended American involvement in Vietnam. By 1975, all American troops were home.

The most scandalous event however, was his attempt to interfere with a police investigation into a burglary at The Watergate Hotel in Washington, D.C. His efforts were really to prevent law enforcement from finding out about quite a few other illegal activities that he had been involved in. After months of investigation, with President Nixon in the news nearly every night, he finally decided to resign. He was the first President in the history of the United States to resign from the presidency.*

The Presidential Footprint

Most historians find President Nixon's years in the White House to be a collection of mixed signals. While his opening up of trade with China was undoubtedly a progressive step, his mistakes in the Watergate scandal won't be forgiven. Many historians point to Nixon's ability to manipulate public opinion for his own political gain. For this, he caused a deep-seated distrust of government to spring up in the United States.

*For comprehension and vocabulary work, see the *Discussion Guide*, page 57.

Birth: January 9, 1913   **Place:** Yorba Linda, California   **Occupation:** Lawyer, Public Official

Religion: Quaker   **Term of Office:** 1969 to 1974   **Death:** April 22, 1994

Position on Civil Rights and Immigration: When Martin Luther King was arrested in 1960, near the end of the presidential campaign, Richard Nixon was silent on the event, while his opponent, John F. Kennedy, phoned King's wife and helped get Reverend King out of jail.

- President Nixon supported anti-busing legislation.
- President Nixon restored more rights to Native Americans than any other president in history.

The Vietnam War

Americans who support the war in Vietnam march in New York City, 1967.

Black Americans protested against the high percentage of young black men who were drafted.

Photo Credit: Library of Congress, Prints & Photographs Division, photograph by Bernard Gotfryd, [Reproduction number e.g., LC-USZ62-123456]; Collection of the Smithsonian National Museum of African American History and Culture 1971-1972

A crowd of protesters against the Vietnam War gather in a park in New York City in the rain.

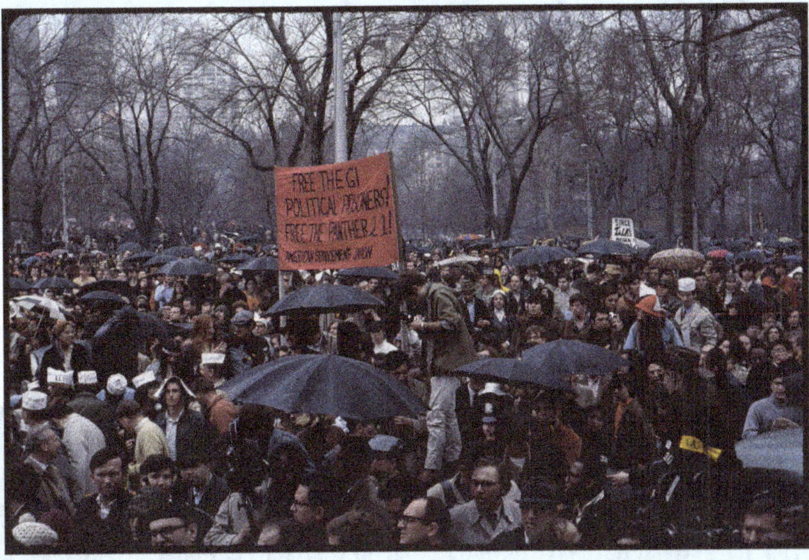

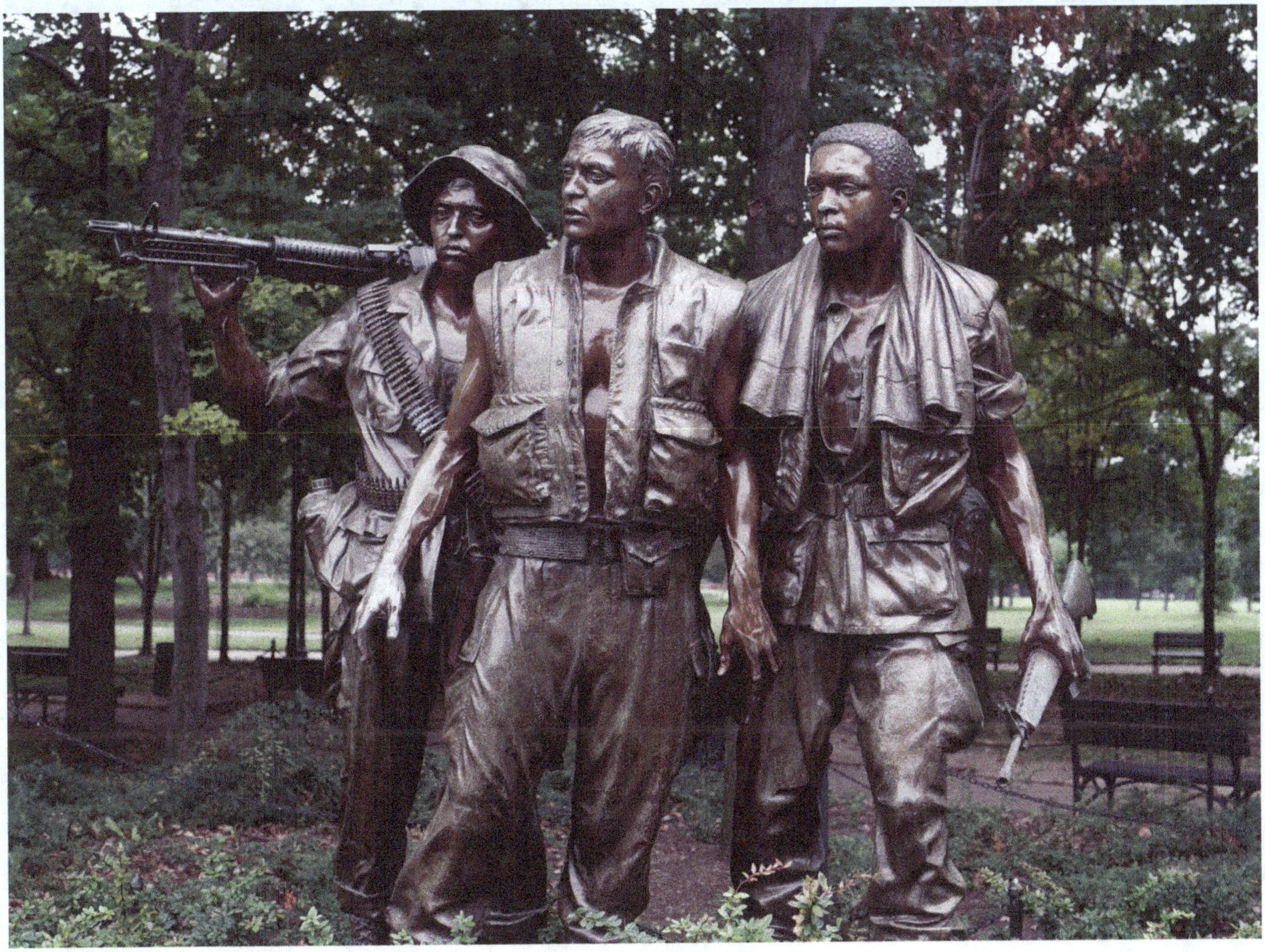

Vietnam Memorial Soldiers, on the Mall in Washington, D.C.

Photo Credit: Gotfryd, Bernard, photographer. Anti-Vietnam war rally New York. United States New York, 1969. [April] Photograph. https://www.loc.gov/item/2020737982/.; Carol M. Highsmith's America, Library of Congress, Prints and Photographs Division.

Gerald R. Ford

Choosing a Name

Gerald Ford was born as Leslie Lynch King, Jr., But his mom divorced her husband and moved to Michigan when Leslie was an infant. There she married Gerald Rudolph Ford, a merchant. The family was a happy one, so his mother called her son Jerry after her new husband. Upon graduation from college, Leslie officially and affectionately changed his name to Gerald Rudolph Ford, after the only father he ever knew.

In high school, he loved history and participated in school government. Jerry also played center on the football team and became one of the best players in the state. He was smart, graduating in the top 5% of his class, and well-liked, voted the most popular. His football skills took him to the University of Michigan where he played center and was voted MVP.

38th President of the United States

Working His Way Through College

Even though he had to work at several jobs to pay for college, he still turned down a spot on the Green Bay Packers. He was also offered a position with the Detroit Lions, but he wanted to go to law school. So, he accepted a job as a football coach for Yale, hoping that they would get to know him and accept him into their law school. After three years, they accepted him on probation, and he graduated in 1941.

Back in Michigan, he was active in the local Republican party trying to rout the entrenched Republican machine. After the attack on Pearl Harbor, he enlisted in the Navy and served four years in the Pacific theater earning ten battle stars.

In 1948, he won his first of twelve consecutive terms representing Michigan in the U.S. House of Representatives. He quickly became known as a hard-working, honest young Congressman and was appointed to the powerful Appropriations Committee, which allocates government funding.

Other Republicans trusted him, so when President Nixon's Vice President resigned under a cloud of corruption, Nixon chose Gerald Ford to replace him. When the Watergate scandal forced President Nixon to resign, Ford took the oath of office and became President on August 9, 1974. He was the first person in history to serve as Vice President and President without ever having been elected to either office.

President Gerald R. Ford

Shortly into his term, President Ford issued a presidential pardon to Richard Nixon. It was a controversial move because many Americans wanted him punished. For a congressman who had previously enjoyed great popularity, he was suddenly facing harsh criticism. Some worried that he had made a deal with Nixon before he resigned, so a congressional committee investigated and concluded that there had been no deal. Only two months into Ford's presidency, his reputation seemed to be irreparable.

President Ford struggled throughout the rest of his two-year term. The country was suffering from inflation, or uncontrollable rising prices, as well as unemployment. Ford was not successful in improving either one. In addition, he faced rising oil prices, an economic crisis in New York City, and a desegregation problem in Boston that threatened to explode into rioting.

On the international front, he managed to close out the Vietnam war, but experienced mixed successes and stalls with the Soviet Union. In all, it was a difficult two years. The public seemed to agree and did not re-elect him.*

The Presidential Footprint

President Ford faced national issues that no other President had faced: he took over from a president who had resigned and he faced economic issues that were difficult even for the brightest advisors of the day. With a Democratic-controlled Congress, he was facing a deck that seemed to be stacked against him. However, to the present day, historians and Americans alike believe that Gerald R. Ford was a decent and honest man who restored honor to the presidency.

*For comprehension and vocabulary work, see the *Discussion Guide*, page 58.

Birth: July 14, 1913   **Place:** Omaha, Nebraska   **Occupation:** Lawyer, Public Official

Religion: Episcopalian   **Term of Office:** 1974 to 1977   **Death:** December 26, 2006

Position on Civil Rights and Immigration: While Gerald Ford played football at the University of Michigan, Georgia Tech came in town for a game. They demanded that Michigan bench their only Black American player. He was a friend of Ford's, who demanded that they let him play. But his friend asked Ford to play and hit them hard for him. So he did, and it was the only win that season for the University of Michigan.

- He signed an amendment to the Voting Rights Act of 1965.

- He did not intervene in Boston's struggle to integrate their schools, believing that it was up to the states to solve their own problems.

James E. Carter, Jr.

Pulling Out of Poverty

In 1924, James Earl Carter was born in a hospital and raised in a rural home without electricity or running water. His parents were peanut farmers who owned a warehouse and a store. They worked hard and earned a modest living. Young Jimmy helped by taking farm goods to sell in the town market. During the Depression, he saved enough money to buy five abandoned houses in town and rented them out.

With an uncle in the Navy, the family received postcards from all over the world, and Jimmy dreamed of following in his footsteps. Before he was in high school, he applied for brochures from the Naval Academy in Annapolis, Maryland. But during World War II, competition for entry into the Academy was fierce. While waiting for an acceptance letter, Jimmy attended the Georgia Institute of Technology and finally entered the Naval Academy in 1943. He graduated with honors in 1946, one year after the war ended.

39th President of the United States

Volunteering and Teaching

To start his naval career, he volunteered for the Navy's most dangerous work, the new fleet of nuclear submarines. On the leading research team, he taught nuclear engineering to the crew. But by 1953, he had to leave the Navy and return home to save the farm. His father was dying of cancer.

Assisting the Civil Rights Movement

In 1954, a cultural shudder shook the South when the Supreme Court ruled that segregation in schools was unconstitutional. By then, Carter was succeeding with the farm. So he began serving on community boards and won election to the local Board of Education in 1955. In 1962, he served in the State Senate, working to reform laws that discouraged Black Americans from voting.

Because he was a liberal Democrat, his beliefs were a disadvantage in Georgia during these early days of the civil rights movement. During his campaign for governor, he learned to cut back on appearances to black churches. He won by a slim margin. In his inaugural address, he announced that it was time to end segregation in the state. As governor, he reformed government processes and hired more Black Americans into government positions.

Entering Rough Waters in Washington, D.C.

James Earl Carter was an uncommon Southern politician. He was not a party-machine politician. And he brought to the White House a carefully crafted informal tone and hoped to avoid some common practices in Washington. For example, he objected to "pork barrel" projects, or add-ons to laws that gave congressmen government-funded projects for their districts. He lost many of those fights with Congress.

They fought back by refusing to pass his suggested laws for consumer protection and workers' reform. The President, in turn, refused to sign a bill that Congress passed to increase public works repair and building. The stage was set for a feisty relationship.

Enjoying Some Mixed Success

Carter did succeed in creating the Department of Energy, which sponsored research into alternative fuels. He also signed laws to de-regulate oil and natural gas prices. Ultimately, this increased the United States' own fuel production, and prices were lowered. But none of this happened before foreign oil nations increased their prices so high that Americans were struggling to pay for gas. His approval ratings plummeted.

However, he had one notable success in foreign policy. He negotiated a peace treaty between Egypt and Israel, for which the two signing Presidents won the Nobel Prize. Yet his worst failure was also in foreign policy, when a militant group in Iran took over the American Embassy and held sixty-six Americans hostage. For over a year, Carter was unable to free them despite secret negotiations. On his last day in office after Reagan was sworn in, the militants released the hostages.*

The Presidential Footprint

Jimmy Carter was not re-elected in 1980. Although many historians felt he was a better former-President than he was a President, some historians are reviewing his record. They are now pointing out that it was Carter who first began de-regulating industry (not Reagan). The discussions are ongoing, and it remains to be seen what legacy future historians will assign to Jimmy Carter.

*For comprehension and vocabulary work, see the *Discussion Guide*, page 59.

Birth: October 1, 1924 **Place:** Plains, Georgia **Occupation:** Soldier, Farmer, Warehouseman, Public Official, Professor

Religion: Baptist **Term of Office:** 1977 to 1981 **Death:**

Position on Civil Rights and Immigration: After World War II, he served with a mixed-race submarine crew who were invited to a whites-only party. Jimmy persuaded them not to attend.

- White citizens of Plains formed the White Citizens Council as a reaction against the growing civil rights movement. Despite pressure to join, Jimmy Carter was the lone holdout, even when the town boycotted his business. Despite near bankruptcy, he refused to join the whites-only council, and the boycott eventually dissolved.

- In the early 1960s when his Plains Baptist church voted whether to integrate, he and his wife were two of three people who voted in favor of it.

Ronald W. Reagan

Growing Up in the Midwest

Ronald Reagan grew up in Dixon, Illinois during the 1920s and 1930s. His mother was a religious woman who volunteered in prisons, poorhouses, and hospitals. She taught her two sons to forgive their father, who was an alcoholic. While he struggled with alcoholism, he was the local Director of the Depression-era government program, the Works Progress Administration, which provided jobs for the locally unemployed.

40th President of the United States

Young Ronald played both football and basketball in high school. He was active in the theater group and was elected president of the student body. He also spent summers working as a lifeguard on the Rock River, which was known to be quite dangerous. Newspapers often reported him saving people in the river, and later researchers confirmed that he saved about seventy-seven people.

He graduated from high school in 1928, about fourteen months before the great stock market crash of 1929. He went to Eureka College and graduated in 1932 with a "C" average. Though he was not academically brilliant, he was socially active. He joined the drama club and was a member of both the football and swim teams. He was also active in the debate club, on the yearbook staff, on the campus newspaper, and was president of the student council.

Working in the Entertainment Industry

Although he studied economics in college, he got a job as a radio sportscaster in Davenport, Iowa. His years in drama club developed his natural vocal ability, and he began doing sportscasts of major college football games. When he went to California in 1937 to report on spring training for the Chicago Cubs, he was "discovered" by Warner Brothers. He began making "B" movies, or below top-level in popularity. Nevertheless, he made a good living and worked steadily from 1937 to 1957, making more than 50 movies.

When Japan attacked Pearl Harbor in 1941, he was called to active duty as a second lieutenant. Since he was nearsighted, he never saw combat, but they put

Reagan as a lifeguard

him to work narrating combat training films. In 1954, General Electric hired him to host a Sunday night television series called General Electric Theater. When that show lost its popularity, he signed on to film a western.

Beginning as a Democrat

During the Great Depression, Reagan's parents were loyal supporters of Democratic President Franklin Delano Roosevelt. Young Ronald found FDR's optimism infectious, and it confirmed his own natural optimism. As an adult, he continued to identify with Democratic goals. Yet as President of the Screen Actors' Guild, he worried about the anti-Communist uproar from Washington, as the Committee on Un-American Activities focused on finding communists in Hollywood. He had secretly worked undercover for the FBI to locate communists. But later, he sought to clear the names of many whom he believed had been falsely accused.

The Reagan family, Ronald as the youngest

But when the Republican candidate, Eisenhower, ran for the presidency in 1952, Reagan joined a "Democrats for Eisenhower" group. It was his first move into Republican territory, where he ultimately stayed.

Developing Compromise Skills as Governor

In 1967, he began his first term as Governor of California, and he was re-elected to a second term in 1971. His friendliness proved to be an asset in the Governor's office, as he had a knack for bringing opponents to a compromise. One of his lasting achievements was the passage of the Welfare Reform Act (1971). This revision of the California welfare programs restricted the eligibility requirements, but increased benefits.

Governor Reagan also approved the establishment of Redwood National Park, north of San Francisco. To preserve the area, he also refused approval of a dam in the area and signed a bill to protect rivers in northern California and historic nature trails.

Becoming President Reagan

When Reagan took the presidential oath of office, he stated the theme of his conservative presidency in his inaugural address. He explained that he was not against the government, but that he proposed "to make it work—work with us, not over us; to stand by our side, not ride on our backs."

As he settled down to work, he showed that as governor he had learned the art of compromise when he appointed James A. Baker III to be White House Chief of Staff. Baker had managed two campaigns for Reagan's political opponents. The appointment revealed Reagan's friendly nature, and his recognition of the need for compromise.

Implementing Trickle-Down Economics

President Reagan named the economy as his first order of business. He became known for supporting a theory called "supply-side economics." It theorized that if suppliers, businesses and the wealthy, would be taxed less, then the money they kept would be spent in ways that created jobs for others. It was often called "trickle-down" economics because extra funds should "drip" down, through spending, to members of society who earned less money.

At first, the theory did not work, and the country's unemployment increased. By 1984, Reagan signed the Tax Equity and Fiscal Responsibility Act, which was a balance of tax cuts and increases. While economists disagree about what caused it, the country experienced an economic boom in the 1980s.

During his second term as President, Reagan continued to make the economy the center of his program. In 1986 he signed the Tax Reform Act, which closed some businesses' tax loopholes and raised taxes on other businesses.

Many Americans were angry when Reagan fired eleven thousand air traffic controller union workers. Reagan argued that since they were government employees, they had no right to strike.

Taking a Strong Stance in Cold War Strategy

Since the 1950s communist scare, Ronald Reagan had been against communism. By 1983, he believed that military strength was a deterrent to the Soviet Union's world influence. To that end, he approved $220 billion in military spending. Part of that would be spent on a shield in outer space that would protect the U.S. from incoming missiles. The science of this defense was not proven, yet Reagan wanted the research to begin.

In June 1987, Reagan continued this tough stance when he was scheduled to make a speech in Berlin for the 750th anniversary of the founding of the city. After World War II, the Soviets had built a concrete wall separating East from West Berlin. It became a symbol of the Cold War, or the tension between the Soviets in the East, and Europe with the U.S. in the West. In Reagan's speech, he uttered the now-famous line, addressed to

Reagan and Gorbachev

Gorbachev, the leader of the Soviet Union, "Tear down this wall!" Although it took two and a half years, the state council of East Germany ultimately allowed citizens to dismantle it, and Germans were finally free to move about the city.*

The Presidential Footprint

President Reagan's admirers call him "The Great Communicator." Many historians agree that he was very effective at speech-making and persuasion. But they also point out that he was a politician who wanted success, even if it meant he would have to compromise. They point to his welfare reform bill from his Governor years as his biggest achievement, and it included some significant compromises. He was a popular President. Even today, many members of Congress identify themselves as Reagan Republicans.

For comprehension and vocabulary work, as well as a mini lesson on the Berlin Wall, see the *Discussion Guide*, pages 60-62.

Birth: February 6, 1911   **Place:** Tampico, Illinois   **Occupation:** Actor, Public Official

Religion: Christian Church   **Term of Office:** 1981 to 1989   **Death:** June 5, 2004

Position on Civil Rights and Immigration: Candidate Reagan said in a speech delivered in Mississippi, near the town where three civil rights workers had been murdered, that he believed in "states' rights." It was considered code language allowing local authorities to "deal with" civil rights issues as they saw fit.

- Early in the 1960s, he was opposed to the Civil Rights Act of 1964. Although later in his political career, he came to support it.

- He signed a bill that gave amnesty to Mexican Americans. And he signed a bill that created Martin Luther King Day.

The Berlin Wall

President Kennedy addressed West Berliners in 1963, in which he delivered a now-famous line in German, expressing solidarity with them. "Ich bin ein Berliner!" Translated, it says: "I am a Berliner!" June 26, 1963.

President Nixon points to areas in East Berlin over the wall, February 27, 1969.

Vice President Bush tours the Berlin Wall on January 31, 1983.

President Reagan delivers a speech at the Brandenburg Gate of the Berlin Wall on June 12, 1987, in which he famously challenged Premier Gorbachev, "Mr. Gorbachev, Tear down this wall!"

George H. W. Bush

Starting Out on the East Coast

George Herbert Walker Bush came from a wealthy family, whose father was an investment banker and who served Connecticut as their U.S. Senator from 1952 to 1963. Young Bush attended a private school in Massachusetts called Phillips Academy Andover. During his senior year, he was elected Class President and enlisted in the Navy as soon as he graduated in 1942.

He was the youngest pilot in the Navy and flew torpedo bombers on fifty-eight combat missions. On one mission, he was shot down and rescued by an American submarine. For his bravery, he was awarded the Distinguished Flying Cross.

41st President of the United States

Moving to the Oil Industry

After the war, he studied at Yale University and majored in economics. He and his wife Barbara moved to Texas in 1948, where he worked in the oil industry. Eventually, he and a friend formed a company that manufactured oil drilling equipment.

In 1966, he campaigned for the U.S. House of Representatives and won. After serving two terms, he ran for the Senate and lost. But President Nixon had noticed the young congressman and appointed him to be ambassador to the United Nations. After three years, President Nixon asked him to be chairman of the Republican National Committee, where he earned respect as an honest and dependable leader.

Leading the National Republican Party

When President Nixon became embroiled in the Watergate scandal, Bush told him that he had lost the trust of the Republican party. The new president, Ford, appointed Bush to be envoy to the People's Republic of China, and then in 1975, as the director of the Central Intelligence Agency (CIA), the department that gathers information about other countries. But during the Carter presidential years, Bush returned to Houston.

In 1980, candidate Ronald Reagan chose him to be his Vice President, and he spent the next eight years in that role. He represented the Reagan administration in many international roles, a job that proved to be beneficial when he became president. His promise to carry forward Reagan politics was his main appeal to the voters.

Reaching Compromises

Partly because of the increased military spending of President Reagan, President Bush faced a $2.8 trillion dollar government debt. To solve the problem, the Republicans in Congress proposed severe spending cuts. While the Democrats sought to tax the wealthiest Americans. As with many problems that Washington faces, a solution was reached through compromise. President Bush signed the Omnibus Budget Reconciliation Act of 1990, which raised taxes and cut many items out of the budget.

Regulating Employment and the Environment

Two other major accomplishments during Bush's presidency were the Americans with Disabilities Act and the Clean Air Act. The first law required employers to consider persons with disabilities for jobs. It also required equal access to public transportation, public buildings, and communications equipment. Although many people thought that the law intruded into private affairs, the president pointed out that when people with disabilities become employed, they could be taken off welfare.

The Clean Air Act added to previous environmental laws passed in 1963, 1970, and 1977. This time around, the law required the clean-up of city air pollution, and it cleaned up industrial emissions creating "acid rain" that was killing large areas of forests.

Developing "A New World Order"

In foreign affairs, President Bush proved to be a decisive leader when he ordered 23,000 troops to put down a military revolt in Panama. They had killed an American soldier and attacked another after a military dictator had taken over the country. The Americans arrested the dictator and brought him to the United States to face trial.*

The Presidential Footprint

Bush may be best remembered for his ability to create a multinational coalition of troops to fight against Iraq. The Iraqi leader had invaded its neighbor, Kuwait, and the international community fought back. In fact, the U.S., Great Britain, and the Soviet Union united in publicly condemning Iraq's invasion. Many credit this moment as the true end of the decades-long Cold War. The international troops successfully forced Iraq out, and President Bush heralded a "new world order."

*For comprehension and vocabulary work, see the *Discussion Guide*, page 63.

Birth: June 12, 1924 **Place:** Milton, Massachusetts **Occupation:** Businessman, Public Official

Religion: Episcopalian **Term of Office:** 1989 to 1993 **Death:** November 30, 2018

Position on Civil Rights and Immigration: Many Americans took offense when candidate Bush called his grandchildren the "little brown ones" because his daughter-in-law was born in Mexico. He defended the remark as a term of endearment and later made a campaign ad with his grandchildren.

- He appointed Black American Colin Powell to a top post in the military and Dr. Louis Sullivan of the Morehouse School of Medicine (Black college in Atlanta) to be the Secretary of Health and Human Services.

- He supported President Johnson's civil rights programs, which was unusual for a Congressman from the South.

William J. Clinton

Growing Up with Strong Women

William Clinton was born in Hope, Arkansas in 1946. He enjoyed attending his local Baptist church, though some say it may have been mostly for his love of gospel music. He was also raised by his grandmother and mother, two strong women who argued often.

His high school was run by Principal Johnny Mae Mackey who counseled Bill to follow his dreams of public service. To that end, he attended an American Legion convention in Washington, D.C., called Boy's Nation. While there, he shook hands with President Kennedy. The photo capturing the moment is often pointed to as prophetic of Bill's future role.

42nd President of the United States

Heading for Public Service

Whether it was prophecy or encouragement, young Bill was interested in public service. He went to Georgetown University and studied International Affairs. Although many classmates saw him as a backwards country boy, he was ambitious and outgoing, qualities that helped him win elections for class president. By his third year, he lost the election and learned a valuable lesson. He had tried to please everyone, and in the end, people did not trust him.

Yet he was a brilliant student and in his third year got a job clerking for the U.S. Senate Foreign Relations Committee. He won a Rhodes scholarship to study for two years at Oxford University in England as well. Although he was drafted to serve in Vietnam, he was allowed to finish his studies at Oxford. When he re-submitted his name, he was never called to duty.

Starting His Career in Law and Government

Upon graduation, he went home to teach law at the University of Arkansas. He immediately began running for office—for the U.S. House of Representatives—a race he lost. But only two years later, he was elected attorney general for Arkansas. Then at age 32, he became the youngest governor Arkansas ever had.

However, his inexperience showed, and he was not re-elected. But in a few years, he was back campaigning. He charmingly admitted his past mistakes, and voters gave him a second chance, and a third, and a fourth. He championed many reforms and became known nationally as a reform Democrat, even though his speeches placed him squarely in the center of political theories, as a centrist.

Defining the Middle-of-the-Road for Democrats

Some say that President Clinton remade the Democratic party by promoting middle-of-the-road views, rather than the extremely liberal views that some Democrats were embracing. His focus for his first term was the economy, which could not be separated from the international business world.

He is most known for reducing the huge federal deficit, inherited from the previous administration. Simultaneously, the booming economy gave the government an extra $124 billion in tax revenue. Overall, the government operated with extra money. During the Clinton years, the American economy was the strongest in the world.

In many cases, Clinton supported Republican-led programs, like the North Atlantic Free Trade Agreement (NAFTA). This allowed trade without taxes between Canada, the United States, and Mexico. But his biggest push—for a national healthcare system—failed. In addition, he was the second President in history to be impeached. Although the effort to remove him from office failed, the scandals that led to impeachment sullied his reputation.

Succeeding in Foreign Policy

Despite his problems at home, President Clinton was able to ease the world's nuclear fears. In improving the relationship with the Soviet Union, Clinton's state department led the effort to dismantle nuclear weapons in the former Soviet Union and to install safeguards for nuclear power plants. It has been said that this achievement made the world a safer place and was one more indication of the end of the Cold War.*

The Presidential Footprint

President Clinton's time in office is too recent for many scholars to reach conclusions about his effectiveness. Though many historians are studying his ability to balance the federal budget and support a booming economy to determine how much of that success can really be credited to his own policies. The discussions between historians have just begun.

*For comprehension and vocabulary work, see the *Discussion Guide*, page 64.

Birth: August 19, 1946　　**Place:** Hope, Arkansas　　**Occupation:** Lawyer, Public Official

Religion: Baptist　　**Term of Office:** 1993 to 2001　　**Death:**

Position on Civil Rights and Immigration: He appointed more women, Black Americans, and Latinx professionals to highly visible government positions than any previous president.

- He received the NAACP Legal Defense and Education Fund Lifetime Achievement Award in 2001.

- As recognition for his commitment to civil rights, he received the Joint Center for Political and Economic Studies' Louis E. Martin Great American Award in 2006.

George W. Bush

Growing Up in the Suburbs

George W. Bush grew up in Midland, Texas, a small city in west Texas. While his dad worked in the oil industry, young George grew up as a typical post-war baby in a suburb filled with children. But in 1953, when he was only seven, his four-year-old sister died of leukemia. The loss was a sudden and profound blow. The closeness he developed with his mother during this time remained with him, even after the next four siblings came along.

He attended a public elementary school, but for high school, he went to the same private school his dad had attended, Phillips Academy Andover in Massachusetts. The coursework was hard, and he was not a brilliant student. But he worked diligently, well past the "lights-out" time in the dormitory. He was, however, good at making friends and had many. They proved to be a solid support for him so far from his Texas home.

43rd President of the United States

Campaigning for His Dad

During his freshman year at Yale University, his dad ran for the U.S. Senate, and young George helped on the campaign. Although his dad lost the election, son George gained valuable insights into the democratic process. In addition to his extracurricular campaigning for his dad, he studied history and played on the baseball and rugby teams. After graduation, he served in the Air National Guard, training at the Moody Air Force Base in Georgia. And later, he earned a Masters in Business Administration from Harvard.

He was a successful businessman when he decided to run for Governor of Texas and defeated a popular and longtime governor. He succeeded in reforming education in the state and acquired a national reputation for his work.

Leading the Nation against Terrorism

Only about eight months into his presidency, the country experienced the most devastating terrorist attack in its history. Early in the morning of September 11, 2001, while President Bush was visiting a school in Florida, two commercial airplanes were hijacked and flew into the World Trade Center in Manhattan. A little later, a third hijacked plane crashed into the Pentagon in Washington. A fourth plane crashed into a field in Pennsylvania after passengers overtook the hijackers and forced it down.

During what could be argued as the worst day in U.S. history, President Bush projected a sense of calm. During the day, he worked behind the scenes with the military, his secretary of state, and national security advisors to plan a response. Later that evening, he addressed the American people. He announced that "We will make no distinction between the terrorists who committed these acts and those who harbor them." He closed his remarks with a quote from Psalms and set the following Friday as a National Day of Prayer and Remembrance.

Tracking Down Terrorists and Making Mistakes

The country was at war against terrorism. The first focus was to track down the terrorists who were believed to be hiding in Afghanistan. This war was to become the longest in the nation's history.

Although the 9/11 attacks distracted Bush from his education goals, he carried with him a plan, similar to the one he pushed through in Texas, to reform education nationally. He signed the No Child Left Behind Act in 2002, which required all students to achieve certain levels of proficiency in math and reading. For the first time in many years, low-income students began to gain ground in these areas.*

The Presidential Footprint

Because President George W. Bush is still living, his legacy is still to be debated during the coming years. Many historians praise his decision to return to Washington on 9/11, despite some advisors urging him to go into hiding. As part of his war on terrorism, he approved an invasion of Iraq in a search for "weapons of mass destruction." Many still feel that this military action was at best misguided, and at worst, a war crime. Also, his No Child Left Behind was replaced by other legislation in 2015.

*For comprehension and vocabulary work, see the *Discussion Guide*, page 65.

Birth: July 6, 1946 **Place:** New Haven, Connecticut **Occupation:** Businessman, Public Official

Religion: Methodist **Term of Office:** 2001 to 2009 **Death:**

Position on Civil Rights and Immigration: President Bush believed that the quiet habit of allowing minority and low-income students to aim low in life was, in fact, what he called the "soft bigotry of low expectations. And for the sake of America's children, that is something we cannot allow."

• The No Child Left Behind Act aimed to level the field for all children in America.

Barack H. Obama

Growing Up in Hawaii and Indonesia

Barack Obama's parents were students at the University of Hawaii when they met and married. Their first son, Barack, was born on August 4, 1961 in Honolulu. His mother was from Kansas, and his father was an international student from Kenya. They divorced when Barack was only two, and he and his mother traveled to Indonesia where she continued her studies in cultural anthropology. She eventually earned a PhD. in anthropology, the study of human society and their cultures.

While they lived in Indonesia, Barack attended both Catholic and Muslim schools, though he explained later in life that he never practiced Islam. As he got a little older, his mother sent him back to Hawaii to live with his grandparents and attend a Hawaiian college-preparatory school called Punahou. While he lived with his grandparents, who were non-practicing Methodists and Baptists, Barack has said that he was not raised in a religious household.

44th President of the United States

Learning to be Proud of His Heritage

His mother taught him to be proud of being African, explaining that he was the heir to a great heritage. Although Hawaii at the time was home to a great cultural diversity, it was nevertheless, not home to many African Americans, and young Barack struggled with self-identity.

At eighteen, he went to New York City to attend Columbia University, and graduated in 1983 with a degree in political science. It was when he accepted a job as a community organizer on Chicago's poor South Side that he was finally immersed in his black heritage that he had longed to experience. He worked diligently to organize black residents of the projects to demand better living conditions in the complex. He finally realized that with the Chicago political scene, he would have to have a law degree to be truly useful. He needed a better understanding of the law.

Getting a Law Degree

By 1988, he was attending Harvard Law School. He became the school's first black president of the well-known Harvard Law Review, a student-run magazine of legal scholarly articles. Normally, the magazine is a very conservative publication. Even though Obama was known to be a liberal, he was nevertheless elected President because he promised the student staff that he would be fair-minded toward their conservative views.

As the first black president of the Review, he drew some national attention and was even offered a contract from a large publishing company to write a book. He wrote *Dreams from My Father: A Story of Race and Inheritance*. It explained the difficulties of growing up black, without his black father present, while being raised by white parents and grandparents.

Working to Secure Civil Rights

After graduation, he went back to Chicago to work for a law firm that specialized in civil rights cases. He also became a lecturer for the University of Chicago Law School. He met his future wife, Michelle and they settled in Hyde Park, an integrated neighborhood on the south side of Chicago.

In 1996, his voting district's representative gave up her seat in the Illinois state legislature because she wanted to run for the U.S. Congress. Barack Obama threw his hat into the ring and ran for the state legislature. He won. Over the course of his eight years in the state legislature, he was able to pass about 300 laws that aimed to improve the lives of the poor.

He served in the U.S. Senate as well, from 2005 to 2008. And in 2009, he was inaugurated as America's first black President.

Kids playing at the Ida B. Wells homes in Chicago

Gathering "A Team of Rivals"

One of the first jobs of any president is to appoint professionals to lead the different government agencies in Washington, and to serve as his advisors. This group is called the Presidential Cabinet, and they meet regularly in the White House. He followed what one historian called a "team of rivals" philosophy, used by President Lincoln. That is, Obama kept some members from President Bush's cabinet, and a few others whom he knew would disagree with him on key issues.

Obama sitting on the Rosa Parks bus

Managing through the Great Recession

From the first day of his presidency, Obama walked into the early days of the worst economic recession since the Great Depression. It started at the end of Bush's term as banks were closing, and millions of Americans were losing their homes. President Obama agreed with President Bush's plan, called Troubled Asset Relief Program, and he added $60 billion to Bush's $20 billion assigned to prevent the American car industry from going out of business.

In addition, Obama proposed an $800 billion package called the American Recovery and Reinvestment Act. It gave money to states, so they wouldn't have to lay off employees. It also provided money to fix bridges and roads. Both programs seemed to work and kept the economy from becoming even worse.

Setting Up Health Care for the Uninsured

Yet Obama wanted to follow through on a problem that Democratic Presidents since Harry Truman had been trying to accomplish—the passage of a national health care program. Important laws had already set up portions of health care programs, but President Obama wanted to set up a complete package.

The country had Medicare for the elderly, and Medicaid for the elderly low-income. His idea was a complicated package that would provide "public" health care for everyone. Even though the Democrats controlled the Congress, it was still not an easy law to pass. Yet in March 2010, he signed the Affordable Care Act into law. Almost immediately, Republicans began working to cancel the law, claiming that it was unconstitutional. Although parts of the Act were struck down by the Supreme Court, it remains standing.

President Obama signed the Affordable Care Act on March 23, 2010

Continuing the War Against Terror

President Obama also inherited the role of the United States as leaders in the war against terrorist groups, notably the Taliban. They were assumed to have been the trainers of Al Qaeda, the terrorists who had crashed planes into the World Trade Center. On May 2, 2011, the president approved a plan to have Navy SEALS invade a private home in Pakistan, where the leader of Al Qaeda was believed to be hiding. They succeeded, and Americans were quick to praise the President's decisiveness.*

The Presidential Footprint

Most presidents' legacy only becomes clear many years after the end of their term. It is the same with Barack Obama. Some of his legal victories are under judicial review, and it remains to be seen whether they will stand for future generations. However, many historians point out that his presence in the White House, as the country's first Black American President, is in itself a symbolic legacy that could never be challenged.

Obama and his team listening to an update on Osama bin Laden

*For comprehension and vocabulary work, as well as mini lessons on the Affordable Care Act, and an excerpt from his first inaugural speech, see the *Discussion Guide*, pages 66-68.

Birth: August 4, 1961 **Place:** Honolulu, Hawaii **Occupation:** Community Organizer, Public Official

Religion: Christian **Term of Office:** 2009 to 2017 **Death:**

Position on Civil Rights and Immigration: After graduating from Harvard Law School, he was hired by a law firm in Chicago that specialized in civil rights cases.

- He signed the Affordable Health Care Act into law, giving many low-income Americans access to health care, particularly affecting Black Americans.

- He addressed the Civil Rights Summit in 2014, held at the Lyndon B. Johnson Presidential Library. The event was held in honor of the 50th anniversary of the passing of the Voting Rights Act.

Donald J. Trump

Growing Up in New York City

Mary Anne Trump and her husband Frederick Christ Trump, Sr. lived in a well-to-do neighborhood of Queens in New York City. Frederick Trump was active with the Democratic party in Brooklyn. He also ran a real estate development company that built housing for middle-income white families in Queens, Staten Island, and Brooklyn. Young Donald joined the company when he came of age, working mostly in the construction site offices.

45th President of the United States

His father said later that young Donald was "a pretty rough fellow when he was small." To instill some discipline, his parents enrolled him in the New York Military Academy when he was 13. At age 18, he attended Fordham University and then finished college with a degree in economics from the University of Pennsylvania, in 1968. Although he registered for the draft, he was never called to duty for the Vietnam War.

Joining the Family Business

After graduation, Donald Trump joined his father's business and helped it grow outside the New York area. They bought properties across the country and invested in Manhattan properties. Donald's first successful venture was to develop the Grand Hyatt Hotel in mid-town Manhattan. Although the family company did not have the funds to purchase the hotel, they relied on their father's political connections and Donald's connections with the Hyatt Hotels to secure the deal. Later, the Trump Organization built the Trump Plaza and the Trump Tower, both in Manhattan. Over the next twenty years, they built the Trump Plaza Hotel and Casino, and the Trump Taj Mahal, both as entries into the casino world of Atlantic City, New Jersey.

Steering through Financial Difficulties

During the 1990's, the family experienced severe financial difficulties and began filing for bankruptcy. Throughout the struggle, Donald successfully managed the reconfiguration of several of the family's companies, though the financial struggles continued throughout the next twenty years.

Despite these troubles, Trump was able to maintain his image, or brand, as a successful businessman. He began making money selling his name for use on many businesses: golf courses, hotels, resorts, steaks, and bottled water, to name a few. His brand carried him into a successful run for the White House, proving that many Americans believed in his brand image.

Testing His Successful Brand Image

One of his campaign promises was to "repeal and replace" the Affordable Care Act (sometimes called Obamacare). Although Congress failed to repeal it, the Senate did manage to weaken the law. They eliminated the required tax penalty that Americans would have to pay if they did not sign up for health insurance.

As part of his promise to control illegal immigration, President Trump strengthened about 400 miles of existing fencing along the Mexican-American border. He also built about 50 miles of new barriers along the 2000-mile border.

Managing a Health Crisis

During the final year of President Trump's term, the country suffered a severe outbreak of COVID-19, a flu-like disease that spread throughout the world. Trump is credited with supporting a quick-to-market vaccine. Yet he resisted public policy suggestions that were offered by his own administration's Director of the National Institute of Allergy and Infectious Diseases. This ongoing argument is pointed to by many as one cause of great social discontent.

As a conservative President, Trump made lasting changes to the judicial system by awarding lifetime appointments to more conservative judges than any previous president—four to the Supreme Court. Yet he also became the third President in U.S. history to be impeached, and the only President to be impeached twice.*

The Presidential Footprint

As with any former president who is still living, the legacy of Donald J. Trump is unclear. Historians have only just begun to analyze and discuss his impact. As with his business ventures, Donald Trump has maintained a brand that controlled and reshaped the Republican Party, which many historians began calling "the party of Trump."

*For comprehension and vocabulary work, see the *Discussion Guide*, page 69.

Birth: June 14, 1946   **Place:** New York, New York   **Occupation:** Real Estate Developer, Television Personality

Religion: Presbyterian   **Term of Office:** 2017 to 2021   **Death:**

Position on Civil Rights and Immigration: In 1973, the Trump Organization was charged with discriminating against minorities by refusing to rent property to them. Employees were accused of adding codes to applicants' names to indicate their race and then steering them to "suitable" apartments.

The case was settled after two years with several requirements:

- requiring the Trumps to read the Fair Housing Act
- requiring their organization to place ads notifying the public that all minorities had an equal opportunity to seek housing in their facilities
- requiring their organization to provide weekly listings of all apartment vacancies to the minority-run Urban League of New York, for two years.

In President Trump's autobiography, he states: "In the end the government couldn't prove its case, and we ended up making a minor settlement without admitting any guilt."

Bibliography

George Washington

Chervinsky, Lindsay M. "George Washington: Life Before the Presidency." Miller Center of Public Affairs, University of Virginia. Accessed August 15, 2022. https://millercenter.org/president/washington/impact-and-legacy.

Chervinsky, Lindsay M. "George Washington: Life Before the Presidency." Miller Center of Public Affairs, University of Virginia. Accessed August 15, 2022. https://millercenter.org/president/washington/life-before-the-presidency.

George Washington's Mount Vernon. "How President Washington Made the First Appointments." Accessed August 16, 2022. https://www.mountvernon.org/george-washington/the-first-president/how-president-washington-made-the-first-appointments/.

History.com Editors. "Whiskey Rebellion." History.com. Last modified June 21, 2023. https://www.history.com/topics/early-us/whiskey-rebellion.

Warren, Jack D. "Washington's Journey to Barbados." George Washington's Mount Vernon. Accessed August 15, 2022, https://www.mountvernon.org/george-washington/washingtons-youth/journey-to-barbados/.

White House Historical Association. "George Washington." The White House. Accessed August 15, 2022. https://www.whitehouse.gov/about-the-white-house/presidents/george-washington/.

John Adams

Boston Tea Party. "Early Life of John Adams." Accessed August 17, 2022. https://www.bostonteapartyship.com/john-adams-early-life.

Bill of Rights institute. "John Adams and the Boston Massacre Trial: - Handout A: Narrative." Accessed August 17, 2022. https://billofrightsinstitute.org/activities/john-adams-and-the-boston-massacre-trial-handout-a-narrative.

Chervinsky, Lindsay M. "The Households of President John Adams." White House Historical Association. January 3, 2020. https://www.whitehousehistory.org/the-households-of-john-adams.

Costello, Matthew. "Slave Quarters at Decatur House." White House Historical Association. September 5, 2019. https://www.whitehousehistory.org/decatur-house-slave-quarters.

Miller Center of Public Affairs, University of Virginia. "John Adams." Accessed August 17, 2022. https://millercenter.org/president/adams.

National Parks Service. "John Adams Biography." Last modified March 31, 2012. https://www.nps.gov/adam/john-adams-biography.htm.

Nix, Elizabeth. "7 Famous Mayflower Descendants." History.com. Last modified August 23, 2021. https://www.history.com/news/7-famous-mayflower-descendants.

Taylor, James C. "John Adams: Impact and Legacy." Miller Center of Public Affairs, University of Virginia." Accessed August 17, 2022. https://millercenter.org/president/adams/impact-and-legacy.

Taylor, James C. "John Adams: Life Before the Presidency." Miller Center of Public Affairs, University of Virginia." Accessed August 17, 2022. https://millercenter.org/president/adams/life-before-the-presidency.

White House Historical Association. "John Adams." Accessed August 18, 2022. https://www.whitehousehistory.org/bios/john-adams.

White House Historical Association. "John Adams." The White House. Accessed August 18, 2022. https://www.whitehouse.gov/about-the-white-house/presidents/john-adams/.

Thomas Jefferson

Chew, Elizabeth V. "American Indians." Monticello. December 2002. https://www.monticello.org/research-education/thomas-jefferson-encyclopedia/american-indians/.

Ellis, Joseph J. "Thomas Jefferson." Encyclopedia Britannica. July 4, 2023. https://www.britannica.com/biography/Thomas-Jefferson.

Frankavilla, Lisa. "Jefferson, Thomas and His Family." Encyclopedia Virginia. December 7, 2020. https://encyclopediavirginia.org/entries/jefferson-thomas-and-his-family/.

History.com Editors. "Thomas Jefferson." History.com. Last modified March 22, 2022. https://www.history.com/topics/us-presidents/thomas-jefferson.

Miller Center of Public Affairs, University of Virginia. "Thomas Jefferson." Accessed August 20, 2022. https://millercenter.org/president/jefferson.

Onuf, Peter. "Thomas Jefferson: Domestic Affairs." Miller Center of Public Affairs, University of Virginia. Accessed August 20, 2022. https://millercenter.org/president/jefferson/domestic-affairs.

Onuf, Peter. "Thomas Jefferson: Impact and Legacy." Miller Center of Public Affairs, University of Virginia. Accessed August 20, 2022. https://millercenter.org/president/jefferson/impact-and-legacy.

Onuf, Peter. "Thomas Jefferson: Life Before the Presidency." Miller Center of Public Affairs, University of Virginia. Accessed August 20, 2022. https://millercenter.org/president/jefferson/life-before-the-presidency.

Ragosta, John A. "Virginia Statue for Religious Freedom." Monticello. February 21, 2018. https://www.monticello.org/research-education/thomas-jefferson-encyclopedia/virginia-statute-religious-freedom/.

James Madison

Hopkins, Callie. "The Enslaved Household of President James Madison." White House Historical Association. August 28, 2019. https://www.whitehousehistory.org/slavery-in-the-james-madison-white-house#.

Miller Center of Public Affairs, University of Virginia. "James Madison." Accessed August 21, 2022. https://millercenter.org/president/madison.

Stagg, J. C. A. "James Madison: Foreign Affairs." Miller Center of Public Affairs, University of Virginia. Accessed August 21, 2022. https://millercenter.org/president/madison/foreign-affairs.

Stagg, J. C. A. "James Madison: Impact and Legacy." Miller Center of Public Affairs, University of Virginia. Accessed August 21, 2022. https://millercenter.org/president/madison/impact-and-legacy.

Stagg, J. C. A. "James Madison: Life Before the Presidency." Miller Center of Public Affairs, University of Virginia. Accessed August 21, 2022. https://millercenter.org/president/madison/life-before-the-presidency.

White House Historical Association. "James Madison." Accessed August 21, 2022. https://www.whitehousehistory.org/bios/james-madison.

White House Historical Association. "James Madison." The White House. Accessed August 21, 2022. https://www.whitehouse.gov/about-the-white-house/presidents/james-madison/.

James Monroe

Costello, Matthew. "The Enslaved Households of President James Monroe." White House Historical Association. February 25, 2020. https://www.whitehousehistory.org/the-enslaved-households-of-president-james-monroe.

NCC Staff. "10 Birthday Facts About President James Monroe." National Constitution Center. April 28, 2023. https://constitutioncenter.org/blog/10-surprising-birthday-facts-about-james-monroe.

Preston, Daniel. "James Monroe: Impact and Legacy." Miller Center of Public Affairs, University of Virginia.

Accessed August 23, 2022. https://millercenter.org/president/monroe/impact-and-legacy.

Preston, Daniel. "James Monroe: Life Before the Presidency." Miller Center of Public Affairs, University of Virginia. Accessed August 23, 2022. https://millercenter.org/president/monroe/life-before-the-presidency.

The Editors of Encyclopedia Britannica. "Missouri Compromise." Encyclopedia Britannica. Last modified July 17, 2023. https://www.britannica.com/event/Missouri-Compromise.

White House Historical Association. "James Monroe." The White House. Accessed August 23, 2022. https://www.whitehouse.gov/about-the-white-house/presidents/james-monroe/.

John Quincy Adams

History.com Editors. "John Quincy Adams." History.com. Last modified December 3, 2019. https://www.history.com/topics/us-presidents/john-quincy-adams.

Hogan, Margaret A. "John Quincy Adams: Impact and Legacy." Miller Center of Public Affairs, University of Virginia. Accessed August 24, 2022. https://millercenter.org/president/jqadams/impact-and-legacy.

Hogan, Margaret A. "John Quincy Adams: Life Before the Presidency." Miller Center of Public Affairs, University of Virginia. Accessed August 24, 2022. https://millercenter.org/president/jqadams/life-before-the-presidency.

Miller Center of Public Affairs, University of Virginia. "John Quincy Adams." Accessed August 24, 2022. https://millercenter.org/president/jqadams.

White House Historical Association. "John Quincy Adams." The White House. Accessed August 24, 2022. https://www.whitehouse.gov/about-the-white-house/presidents/john-quincy-adams/.

Andrew Jackson

Andrew Jackson's Hermitage. "Presidency." Accessed August 25, 2022. https://thehermitage.com/learn/andrew-jackson/president/presidency.

Feller, Daniel. "Andrew Jackson: Impact and Legacy." Miller Center of Public Affairs, University of Virginia. Accessed August 25, 2022. https://millercenter.org/president/jackson/impact-and-legacy.

Feller, Daniel. "Andrew Jackson: Life Before the Presidency." Miller Center of Public Affairs, University of Virginia. Accessed August 25, 2022. https://millercenter.org/president/jackson/life-before-the-presidency.

Hopkins, Callie. "The Enslaved Household of President Andrew Jackson." White House Historical Association. August 1, 2019. https://www.whitehousehistory.org/slavery-in-the-andrew-jackson-white-house.

Miller Center of Public Affairs, University of Virginia. "Andrew Jackson." Accessed August 25, 2022. https://millercenter.org/president/jackson.

White House Historical Association. "Andrew Jackson." The White House. Accessed August 25, 2022. https://www.whitehouse.gov/about-the-white-house/presidents/andrew-jackson/.

Martin Van Buren

Costello, Matthew. "The Enslaved Households of President Martin Van Buren." White House Historical Association. November 27, 2019. https://www.whitehousehistory.org/the-enslaved-households-of-martin-van-buren.

History.com Editors. "Martin Van Buren." History.com. Last modified May 27, 2020. https://www.history.com/topics/us-presidents/martin-van-buren.

Miller Center of Public Affairs, University of Virginia. "Martin Van Buren." Accessed August 26, 2022. https://millercenter.org/president/vanburen.

Silbey, Joel. "Martin Van Buren: Impact and Legacy." Miller Center of Public Affairs, University of Virginia. Accessed August 26, 2022. https://millercenter.org/president/vanburen/impact-and-legacy.

Silbey, Joel. "Martin Van Buren: Life Before the Presidency." Miller Center of Public Affairs, University of Virginia. Accessed August 26, 2022. https://millercenter.org/president/vanburen/life-before-the-presidency.

White House Historical Association. "Martin Van Buren." The White House. Accessed August 26, 2022. https://www.whitehouse.gov/about-the-white-house/presidents/martin-van-buren/#:~:text=Martin%20Van%20Buren%20was%20the,both%20under%20President%20Andrew%20Jackson.

William Henry Harrison

Freehling, William. "William Harrison: Death of the President." Miller Center of Public Affairs, University of Virginia. Accessed August 28, 2022. https://millercenter.org/president/harrison/death-of-the-president.

Freehling, William. "William Harrison: Impact and Legacy." Miller Center of Public Affairs, University of Virginia. Accessed August 28, 2022. https://millercenter.org/president/harrison/impact-and-legacy.

Freehling, William. "William Harrison: Life Before the Presidency." Miller Center of Public Affairs, University of Virginia. Accessed August 28, 2022. https://millercenter.org/president/harrison/life-before-the-presidency.

White House Historical Association. "William Henry Harrison." White House Historical Association. Accessed August 28, 2022. https://www.whitehousehistory.org/bios/william-henry-harrison#:~:text=As%20a%20slave%20owner%2C%20he,themselves%20should%20decide%20its%20fate.

John Tyler

Costello, Matthew. "The Enslaved Households of President John Tyler." White House Historical Association. January 3, 2020. https://www.whitehousehistory.org/the-enslaved-households-of-president-john-tyler.

Deal, John, and Dictionary of Virginia Biography. "John Tyler (1790-1862)." Encyclopedia Virginia. December 7, 2020. https://encyclopediavirginia.org/entries/tyler-john-1790-1862/.

Freehling, William. "John Tyler: Impact and Legacy." Miller Center of Public Affairs, University of Virginia. Accessed August 29, 2022. https://millercenter.org/president/tyler/impact-and-legacy.

Freehling, William. "John Tyler: Life Before the Presidency." Miller Center of Public Affairs, University of Virginia. Accessed August 29, 2022. https://millercenter.org/president/tyler/life-before-the-presidency.

Miller Center of Public Affairs, University of Virginia. "John Tyler." Accessed August 29, 2022. https://millercenter.org/president/tyler.

James K. Polk

Pinheiro, John C. "James K. Polk: Impact and Legacy." Miller Center of Public Affairs, University of Virginia. Accessed August 30, 2022. https://millercenter.org/president/polk/impact-and-legacy.

Pinheiro, John C. "James K. Polk: Life After the Presidency." Miller Center of Public Affairs, University of Virginia. Accessed August 30, 2022. https://millercenter.org/president/polk/life-after-the-presidency.

Pinheiro, John C. "James K. Polk: Life Before the Presidency." Miller Center of Public Affairs, University of Virginia. Accessed August 30, 2022. https://millercenter.org/president/polk/life-before-the-presidency.

Mann, Lina. "The Enslaved Households of President James K. Polk." White House Historical Association. January 3, 2020. https://www.whitehousehistory.org/the-enslaved-households-of-james-k-polk#:~:text=Polk%20maintained%20a%20different%20public,their%20families%20while%20in%20office.

Miller Center of Public Affairs, University of Virginia. "James K. Polk." Accessed September 1, 2022. https://millercenter.org/president/polk.

Zachary Taylor

Fling, Sarah. "The Enslaved Households of President Zachary Taylor." White House Historical Association. December 9, 2019. https://www.whitehousehistory.org/the-enslaved-households-of-president-zachary-taylor#:~:text=A%20slave%20owner%20himself%2C%20President,following%20the%20 Mexican%2DAmerican%20War.

Holt, Michael. "Zachary Taylor: Campaigns and Elections." Miller Center of Public Affairs, University of Virginia. Accessed September 2, 2022. https://millercenter.org/president/taylor/campaigns-and-elections.

Holt, Michael. "Zachary Taylor: Death of the President." Miller Center of Public Affairs, University of Virginia. Accessed September 2, 2022. https://millercenter.org/president/taylor/death-of-the-president.

Holt, Michael. "Zachary Taylor: Domestic Affairs." Miller Center of Public Affairs, University of Virginia. Accessed September 2, 2022. https://millercenter.org/president/taylor/domestic-affairs.

Holt, Michael. "Zachary Taylor: Foreign Affairs." Miller Center of Public Affairs, University of Virginia. Accessed September 2, 2022. https://millercenter.org/president/taylor/foreign-affairs.

Holt, Michael. "Zachary Taylor: Impact and Legacy." Miller Center of Public Affairs, University of Virginia. Accessed September 2, 2022. https://millercenter.org/president/taylor/impact-and-legacy.

Holt, Michael. "Zachary Taylor: Life Before the Presidency." Miller Center of Public Affairs, University of Virginia. Accessed September 2, 2022. https://millercenter.org/president/taylor/life-before-the-presidency.

Miller Center of Public Affairs, University of Virginia. "Zachary Taylor." Accessed September 2, 2022. https://millercenter.org/president/taylor.

Millard Fillmore

Holt, Michael. "Millard Fillmore: Campaigns and Elections." Miller Center of Public Affairs, University of Virginia. Accessed September 3, 2022. https://millercenter.org/president/fillmore/campaigns-and-elections.

Holt, Michael. "Millard Fillmore: Domestic Affairs." Miller Center of Public Affairs, University of Virginia. Accessed September 3, 2022. https://millercenter.org/president/fillmore/domestic-affairs.

Holt, Michael. "Millard Fillmore: Impact and Legacy." Miller Center of Public Affairs, University of Virginia. Accessed September 3, 2022. https://millercenter.org/president/fillmore/impact-and-legacy.

Holt, Michael. "Millard Fillmore: Life Before the Presidency." Miller Center of Public Affairs, University of Virginia. Accessed September 3, 2022. https://millercenter.org/president/fillmore/life-before-the-presidency.

Miller Center of Public Affairs, University of Virginia. "Millard Fillmore." Accessed September 3, 2022. https://millercenter.org/president/fillmore.

Franklin Pierce

Baker, Jean H. "Franklin Pierce: Campaigns and Elections." Miller Center of Public Affairs, University of Virginia. Accessed September 4, 2022. https://millercenter.org/president/pierce/campaigns-and-elections.

Baker, Jean H. "Franklin Pierce: Domestic Affairs." Miller Center of Public Affairs, University of Virginia. Accessed September 4, 2022. https://millercenter.org/president/pierce/domestic-affairs.

Baker, Jean H. "Franklin Pierce: Impact and Legacy." Miller Center of Public Affairs, University of Virginia. Accessed September 4, 2022. https://millercenter.org/president/pierce/impact-and-legacy.

Baker, Jean H. "Franklin Pierce: Life Before the Presidency." Miller Center of Public Affairs, University of Virginia. Accessed September 4, 2022. https://millercenter.org/president/pierce/life-before-the-presidency.

National Governors Association. "Gov. Benjamin Pierce." Accessed September 4, 2022. https://www.nga.org/governor/benjamin-pierce/.

Miller Center of Public Affairs, University of Virginia. "Franklin Pierce." Accessed September 4, 2022. https://millercenter.org/president/pierce.

James Buchanan

Cooper, William. "James Buchanan: Impact and Legacy." Miller Center of Public Affairs, University of Virginia. Accessed September 5, 2022. https://millercenter.org/president/buchanan/impact-and-legacy.

Cooper, William. "James Buchanan: Life Before the Presidency." Miller Center of Public Affairs, University of Virginia. Accessed September 5, 2022. https://millercenter.org/president/buchanan/life-before-the-presidency.

Eschner, Kat. "President James Buchanan Directly Influenced the Outcome of the Dred Scott Decision." Smithsonian Magazine. March 6, 2017. https://www.smithsonianmag.com/smart-news/president-james-buchanan-directly-influenced-outcome-dred-scott-decision-180962329/.

Leon, Daniel. "The Households of James Buchanan." White House Historical Association. October 13, 2022. https://www.whitehousehistory.org/the-households-of-james-buchanan.

Pennsylvania Department of Conservation and Natural Resources. "History of James Buchanan's Birthplace State Park." Accessed September 5, 2022. https://www.dcnr.pa.gov/StateParks/FindAPark/BuchanansBirthplaceStatePark/Pages/History.aspx.

Urofsky, Melvin I. "Dred Scott Decision." Encyclopedia Britannica. Last modified June 28, 2023. https://www.britannica.com/event/Dred-Scott-decision.

Abraham Lincoln

Burlingame, Michael. "Abraham Lincoln: Impact and Legacy." Miller Center of Public Affairs, University of Virginia. Accessed September 6, 2022. https://millercenter.org/president/lincoln/impact-and-legacy.

Burlingame, Michael. "Abraham Lincoln: Life Before the Presidency." Miller Center of Public Affairs, University of Virginia. Accessed September 6, 2022. https://millercenter.org/president/lincoln/life-before-the-presidency.

Shapel, Benjamin and Willen, Sara. "Abraham Lincoln's Quote About His Mother: "All That I Am or Hope Ever to be, I Get From My Mother." Shapell. May 8, 2012. https://www.shapell.org/historical-perspectives/between-the-lines/mothers-day-hope-ever-get-mother/#:~:text=She%20was%2C%20by%20all%20accounts,he%20might%20lose%20his%20mind.

The Editors of Encyclopedia Britannica. "Lincoln-Douglas Debates." Encyclopedia Britannica. Last modified May 18, 2023. https://www.britannica.com/event/Lincoln-Douglas-debates/additional-info#history.

US National Archives. "White House Kids Series—Robert Todd Lincoln." The Reagan Library Education Blog. April 14, 2023. https://reagan.blogs.archives.gov/2023/04/14/white-house-kids-series-robert-todd-lincoln/#:~:text=The%20eldest%20of%20the%20four,and%20die%20of%20old%20age.

Andrew Johnson

Library of Congress. "Timeline." Accessed September 8, 2022. https://www.loc.gov/collections/andrew-johnson-papers/articles-and-essays/timeline/.

Miller Center of Public Affairs, University of Virginia. "Andrew Johnson." Accessed September 9, 2022. https://millercenter.org/president/johnson.

Varon, Elizaveth R. "Andrew Johnson: Domestic Affairs." Miller Center of Public Affairs, University of Virginia. Accessed September 9, 2022. https://millercenter.org/president/johnson/domestic-affairs.

Varon, Elizaveth R. "Andrew Johnson: Impact and Legacy." Miller Center of Public Affairs, University of Virginia. Accessed September 9, 2022. https://millercenter.org/president/johnson/impact-and-legacy.

Varon, Elizaveth R. "Andrew Johnson: Life Before the Presidency." Miller Center of Public Affairs, University of Virginia. Accessed September 9, 2022. https://millercenter.org/president/johnson/life-before-the-presidency.

Ulysses S. Grant

Miller Center of Public Affairs, University of Virginia. "Ulysses S. Grant." Accessed September 9, 2022. https://millercenter.org/president/grant.

United States House of Representatives: History, Art, and Archives. "The Ku Klux Klan Act of 1871." Accessed September 9, 2022. https://history.house.gov/Historical-Highlights/1851-1900/hh_1871_04_20_KKK_Act/.

Waugh, Joan. "Ulysses S. Grant: Domestic Affairs." Miller Center of Public Affairs, University of Virginia. Accessed September 9, 2022 https://millercenter.org/president/grant/domestic-affairs.

Waugh, Joan. "Ulysses S. Grant: Impact and Legacy." Miller Center of Public Affairs, University of Virginia. Accessed September 9, 2022. https://millercenter.org/president/grant/impact-and-legacy.

Waugh, Joan. "Ulysses S. Grant: Life Before the Presidency." Miller Center of Public Affairs, University of Virginia. Accessed September 9, 2022. https://millercenter.org/president/grant/life-before-the-presidency.

Rutherford B. Hayes

Johnston, Robert D. "Rutherford B. Hayes: Campaigns and Elections." Miller Center of Public Affairs, University of Virginia. Accessed September 10, 2022. https://millercenter.org/president/hayes/campaigns-and-elections.

Johnston, Robert D. "Rutherford B. Hayes: Domestic Affairs." Miller Center of Public Affairs, University of Virginia. Accessed September 10, 2022. https://millercenter.org/president/hayes/domestic-affairs.

Johnston, Robert D. "Rutherford B. Hayes: Impact and Legacy." Miller Center of Public Affairs, University of Virginia. Accessed September 10, 2022. https://millercenter.org/president/hayes/impact-and-legacy.

Johnston, Robert D. "Rutherford B. Hayes: Life Before the Presidency." Miller Center of Public Affairs, University of Virginia. Accessed September 10, 2022. https://millercenter.org/president/hayes/life-before-the-presidency.

James A. Garfield

Gephardt, Alan. "The Most Important Political Change We Have Known': James A. Garfield, Slavery, and Justice in the Civil War Era, Part II." National Parks Service, Garfield Observer. February 2013. https://www.nps.gov/articles/000/-the-most-important-political-change-we-have-known-james-a-garfield-slavery-and-justice-in-the-civil-war-era-part-ii.htm.

Doenecke, Justus. "James A. Garfield: Impact and Legacy." Miller Center of Public Affairs, University of Virginia. Accessed September 11, 2022. https://millercenter.org/president/garfield/impact-and-legacy.

Doenecke, Justus. "James A. Garfield: Life Before the Presidency." Miller Center of Public Affairs, University of Virginia. Accessed September 11, 2022. https://millercenter.org/president/garfield/life-before-the-presidency.

White House Historical Association. "James Garfield." The White House. Accessed September 11, 2022. https://www.whitehouse.gov/about-the-white-house/presidents/james-garfield/#:~:text=As%20the%20last%20of%20the,County%2C%20Ohio%2C%20in%201831.

Chester Arthur

Doenecke, Justus. "Chester A. Arthur: Domestic Affairs." Miller Center of Public Affairs, University of Virginia. Accessed September 12, 2022. https://millercenter.org/president/arthur/domestic-affairs.

Doenecke, Justus. "Chester A. Arthur: Impact and Legacy." Miller Center of Public Affairs, University of Virginia. Accessed September 12, 2022. https://millercenter.org/president/arthur/impact-and-legacy.

Doenecke, Justus. "Chester A. Arthur: Life Before the Presidency." Miller Center of Public Affairs, University of

Virginia. Accessed September 12, 2022. https://millercenter.org/president/arthur/life-before-the-presidency.

Rocca, Mo. "The Black Congressman of Reconstruction: Death of Representation." Paragraphs 6 and 17. Mobituaries. Accessed September 12, 2022. https://mobituaries.com/news/the-podcast/the-black-congressmen-of-reconstruction-death-of-representation/.

Grover Cleveland

Graff, Henry F. "Grover Cleveland: Life Domestic Affairs." Miller Center of Public Affairs, University of Virginia. Accessed September 12, 2022. https://millercenter.org/president/cleveland/domestic-affairs.

Graff, Henry F. "Grover Cleveland: Impact and Legacy." Miller Center of Public Affairs, University of Virginia. Accessed September 12, 2022. https://millercenter.org/president/cleveland/impact-and-legacy.

Graff, Henry F. "Grover Cleveland: Life Before the Presidency." Miller Center of Public Affairs, University of Virginia. Accessed September 12, 2022. https://millercenter.org/president/cleveland/life-before-the-presidency.

Benjamin Harrison

Resnick, Brian and the National Journal. "The Great White House Goat Chase." The Atlantic. May 29, 2015. https://www.theatlantic.com/politics/archive/2015/05/the-great-white-house-goat-chase/454449/.

Spetter, Allan B. "Benjamin Harrison: Campaigns and Elections." Miller Center of Public Affairs, University of Virginia. Accessed September 13, 2022. https://millercenter.org/president/bharrison/campaigns-and-elections.

Spetter, Allan B. "Benjamin Harrison: Impact and Legacy." Miller Center of Public Affairs, University of Virginia. Accessed September 13, 2022. https://millercenter.org/president/cleveland/impact-and-legacy.

Spetter, Allan B. "Benjamin Harrison: Life Before the Presidency." Miller Center of Public Affairs, University of Virginia. Accessed September 13, 2022. https://millercenter.org/president/bharrison/life-before-the-presidency.

Spetter, Allan B. "Benjamin Harrison: Life in Brief." Miller Center of Public Affairs, University of Virginia. Accessed September 13, 2022. https://onedrive.live.com/Edit.aspx?resid=D3A7FA780EF02470!520&wdinitialsession=8a6adec4-7208-4870-b2ab-40c4e7b48860&wdrldsc=20&wdrldc=1&wdrldr=InvalidExternalHyperlinkFailure&wdo=2.

United States House of Representatives: History, Art, and Archives. "The Demise of Reconstruction." Accessed September 13, 2022. https://history.house.gov/Exhibitions-and-Publications/BAIC/Historical-Essays/Temporary-Farewell/Legislative-Interests/.

White House Historical Association. "Benjamin Harrison." Accessed September 13, 2022. https://www.whitehousehistory.org/bios/benjamin-harrison.

William McKinley

Lioudis, Nick. "What Is the Gold Standard? Advantages, Alternatives, and History." Investopedia. Last modified April 30, 2023. https://www.investopedia.com/ask/answers/09/gold-standard.asp.

Gould, Lewis L. "William McKinley: Domestic Affairs." Miller Center of Public Affairs, University of Virginia. Accessed September 14, 2022. https://millercenter.org/president/mckinley/domestic-affairs.

Gould, Lewis L. "William McKinley: Foreign Affairs." Miller Center of Public Affairs, University of Virginia. Accessed September 14, 2022. https://millercenter.org/president/mckinley/foreign-affairs.

Gould, Lewis L. "William McKinley: Impact and Legacy." Miller Center of Public Affairs, University of Virginia. Accessed September 14, 2022. https://millercenter.org/president/mckinley/impact-and-legacy.

Gould, Lewis L. "William McKinley: Life Before the Presidency." Miller Center of Public Affairs, University of Virginia. Accessed September 14, 2022. https://millercenter.org/president/mckinley/life-before-the-presidency.

US National Archives. "Forgotten Legacy: William McKinley, George Henry White, and the Struggle for Black Equality." YouTube. January 29, 2021. https://www.youtube.com/watch?v=O70v7gPqYlw.

Theodore Roosevelt

Milkis, Sidney. "Theodore Roosevelt: Campaigns and Elections." Miller Center of Public Affairs, University of Virginia. Accessed September 14, 2022. https://millercenter.org/president/roosevelt/campaigns-and-elections.

Milkis, Sidney. "Theodore Roosevelt: Domestic Affairs." Miller Center of Public Affairs, University of Virginia. Accessed September 14, 2022. https://millercenter.org/president/roosevelt/domestic-affairs.

Milkis, Sidney. "Theodore Roosevelt: Foreign Affairs." Miller Center of Public Affairs, University of Virginia. Accessed September 14, 2022. https://millercenter.org/president/roosevelt/foreign-affairs.

Milkis, Sidney. "Theodore Roosevelt: Foreign Affairs." Miller Center of Public Affairs, University of Virginia. Accessed September 14, 2022. https://millercenter.org/president/roosevelt/impact-and-legacy.

Milkis, Sidney. "Theodore Roosevelt: Life Before the Presidency." Miller Center of Public Affairs, University of Virginia. Accessed September 14, 2022. https://millercenter.org/president/roosevelt/life-before-the-presidency.

William H. Taft

"Adkins v. Children's Hospital of D. C." Oyez. Accessed September 15, 2022. https://www.oyez.org/cases/1900-1940/261us525.

Arnold, Peri E. "William Taft: Campaigns and Elections." Miller Center of Public Affairs, University of Virginia. Accessed September 15, 2022. https://millercenter.org/president/taft/campaigns-and-elections.

Arnold, Peri E. "William Taft: Domestic Affairs." Miller Center of Public Affairs, University of Virginia. Accessed September 15, 2022. https://millercenter.org/president/taft/domestic-affairs.

Arnold, Peri E. "William Taft: Impact and Legacy." Miller Center of Public Affairs, University of Virginia. Accessed September 15, 2022. https://millercenter.org/president/taft/impact-and-legacy.

Arnold, Peri E. "William Taft: Life Before the Presidency." Miller Center of Public Affairs, University of Virginia. Accessed September 15, 2022. https://millercenter.org/president/taft/life-before-the-presidency.

Bushong, William. "The Life and Presidency of William Howard Taft." White House Historical Association. Accessed September 15, 2022. https://www.whitehousehistory.org/the-life-and-presidency-of-william-howard-taft.

White House Historical Association. "William Howard Taft." The White House. Accessed September 15, 2022. https://www.whitehouse.gov/about-the-white-house/presidents/william-howard-taft/.

Woodrow Willson

Ambar, Saladin. "Woodrow Willson: Domestic Affairs." Miller Center of Public Affairs, University of Virginia. Accessed September 16, 2022. https://millercenter.org/president/wilson/domestic-affairs.

Ambar, Saladin. "Woodrow Willson: Impact and Legacy." Miller Center of Public Affairs, University of Virginia. Accessed September 16, 2022. https://millercenter.org/president/wilson/impact-and-legacy.

Ambar, Saladin. "Woodrow Willson: Foreign Affairs." Miller Center of Public Affairs, University of Virginia. Accessed September 16, 2022. https://millercenter.org/president/wilson/foreign-affairs.

Ambar, Saladin. "Woodrow Willson: Life Before the Presidency." Miller Center of Public Affairs, University of Virginia. Accessed September 16, 2022. https://millercenter.org/president/wilson/life-before-the-presidency.

President Willson House. "Willson and Race." Accessed September 16, 2022. https://woodrowwilsonhouse.org/wilson-topics/wilson-and-race/.

Smithsonian National Postal Museum. "Woodrow Willson: Federal Segregation." Accessed September 16, 2022. https://postalmuseum.si.edu/research-articles/the-history-and-experience-of-african-americans-in-america%E2%80%99s-postal-service-3.

White House Historical Association. "Woodrow Wilsson." Accessed September 16, 2022. https://www.whitehousehistory.org/bios/woodrow-wilson.

Warren G. Harding

History.com Editors. "President Harding Publicly Condemns Lynching." History.com. Last modified October 20, 2020. https://www.history.com/this-day-in-history/harding-publicly-condemns-lynching.

Trani, Eugene P. "Warren G. Harding: Domestic Affairs." Miller Center of Public Affairs, University of Virginia. Accessed September 17, 2022. https://millercenter.org/president/harding/domestic-affairs.

Trani, Eugene P. "Warren G. Harding: Impact and Legacy." Miller Center of Public Affairs, University of Virginia. Accessed September 17, 2022. https://millercenter.org/president/harding/impact-and-legacy.

Trani, Eugene P. "Warren G. Harding: Life Before the Presidency." Miller Center of Public Affairs, University of Virginia. Accessed September 17, 2022. https://millercenter.org/president/harding/life-before-the-presidency.

Calvin Coolidge

Bennings Wallace, Jerry L. "A Biographical Sketch of Calvin Coolidge." Coolidge Foundation. Accessed September 19, 2022. https://coolidgefoundation.org/presidency/a-biographical-sketch-of-calvin-coolidge/.

Coolidge Foundation. "How Did President Coolidge Champion Civil Rights During His Political Career?" Accessed September 19, 2022. https://coolidgefoundation.org/wp-content/uploads/2017/11/President-Coolidge-Civil-Rights.pdf.

Greenberg, David. "Calvin Coolidge: Domestic Affairs." Miller Center of Public Affairs, University of Virginia. Accessed September 19, 2022. https://millercenter.org/president/coolidge/domestic-affairs.

Greenberg, David. "Calvin Coolidge: Impact and Legacy." Miller Center of Public Affairs, University of Virginia. Accessed September 19, 2022. https://millercenter.org/president/coolidge/impact-and-legacy.

Greenberg, David. "Calvin Coolidge: Life Before the Presidency." Miller Center of Public Affairs, University of Virginia. Accessed September 19, 2022. https://millercenter.org/president/coolidge/life-before-the-presidency.

Shogan, Colleen. "Calving Coolidge and Native Americans." White House Historical Association. October 26, 2021. https://www.whitehousehistory.org/calvin-coolidge-and-native-americans.

Herbert Hoover

Hamilton, David E. "Herbert Hoover: Domestic Affairs." Miller Center of Public Affairs, University of Virginia. Accessed September 20, 2022. https://millercenter.org/president/hoover/domestic-affairs.

Hamilton, David E. "Herbert Hoover: Impact and Legacy." Miller Center of Public Affairs, University of Virginia. Accessed September 20, 2022. https://millercenter.org/president/hoover/impact-and-legacy.

Hamilton, David E. "Herbert Hoover: Life Before the Presidency." Miller Center of Public Affairs, University of Virginia. Accessed September 20, 2022. https://millercenter.org/president/hoover/life-before-the-presidency.

Franklin Delano Roosevelt

Leuchtenburg, William E. "Franklin D. Roosevelt: Campaigns and Elections." Miller Center of Public Affairs, University of Virginia. Accessed September 21, 2022. https://millercenter.org/president/fdroosevelt/campaigns-and-elections.

Leuchtenburg, William E. "Franklin D. Roosevelt: Death of the President." Miller Center of Public Affairs, University of Virginia. Accessed September 21, 2022. https://millercenter.org/president/fdroosevelt/death-of-the-president.

Leuchtenburg, William E. "Franklin D. Roosevelt: Domestic Affairs." Miller Center of Public Affairs, University of Virginia. Accessed September 21, 2022. https://millercenter.org/president/fdroosevelt/domestic-affairs.

Leuchtenburg, William E. "Franklin D. Roosevelt: Foreign Affairs." Miller Center of Public Affairs, University of Virginia. Accessed September 21, 2022. https://millercenter.org/president/fdroosevelt/foreign-affairs.

Leuchtenburg, William E. "Franklin D. Roosevelt: Impact and Legacy." Miller Center of Public Affairs, University of Virginia. Accessed September 21, 2022. https://millercenter.org/president/fdroosevelt/impact-and-legacy.

Leuchtenburg, William E. "Franklin D. Roosevelt: Life Before the Presidency." Miller Center of Public Affairs, University of Virginia. Accessed September 20, 2022. https://millercenter.org/president/fdroosevelt/life-before-the-presidency.

Maranzani, Barbara. "10 Things You May Not Know About the Roosevelts." History.com. Last modified October 10, 2019. https://www.history.com/news/10-things-you-may-not-know-about-the-roosevelts.

Harry S. Truman

Hamby, Alonzo L. "Harry S. Truman: Foreign Affairs." Miller Center of Public Affairs, University of Virginia. Accessed September 22, 2022. https://millercenter.org/president/truman/foreign-affairs.

Hamby, Alonzo L. "Harry S. Truman: Impact and Legacy." Miller Center of Public Affairs, University of Virginia. Accessed September 22, 2022. https://millercenter.org/president/truman/impact-and-legacy.

Hamby, Alonzo L. "Harry S. Truman: Life Before the Presidency." Miller Center of Public Affairs, University of Virginia. Accessed September 22, 2022. https://millercenter.org/president/truman/life-before-the-presidency.

National Parks Service. "Harry S. Truman and Civil Rights." Last modified August 18, 2021. https://www.nps.gov/articles/000/harry-s-truman-and-civil-rights.htm#:~:text=Truman%20won%20reelection%2C%20but%20little,end%20segregation%20in%20the%20military.

The Editors of Encyclopedia Britannica. "Postdam Conference." Last Modified July 10, 2023. https://www.britannica.com/event/Potsdam-Conference.

Dwight D. Eisenhower

National Parks Service. "President Eisenhower and Civil Rights." Last modified February 3, 2022. https://www.nps.gov/articles/000/eisenhower-and-civil-rights.htm.

Pach, Chester J. Jr. "Dwight D. Eisenhower: Domestic Affairs." Miller Center of Public Affairs, University of Virginia. Accessed September 23, 2022. https://millercenter.org/president/eisenhower/domestic-affairs.

Pach, Chester J. Jr. "Dwight D. Eisenhower: Foreign Affairs." Miller Center of Public Affairs, University of Virginia. Accessed September 23, 2022. https://millercenter.org/president/eisenhower/foreign-affairs.

Pach, Chester J. Jr. "Dwight D. Eisenhower: Impact and Legacy." Miller Center of Public Affairs, University of Virginia. Accessed September 23, 2022. https://millercenter.org/president/eisenhower/impact-and-legacy.

Pach, Chester J. Jr. "Dwight D. Eisenhower: Life Before the Presidency." Miller Center of Public Affairs, University of Virginia. Accessed September 23, 2022. https://millercenter.org/president/eisenhower/life-before-the-presidency.

John F. Kennedy

John F. Kennedy Presidential Library and Museum. "The Modern Civil Rights Movement and the Kennedy Administration." Accessed September 24, 2022. https://www.jfklibrary.org/learn/about-jfk/jfk-in-history/civil-rights-movement#:~:text=Kennedy%20defined%20the%20civil%20rights,of%20the%20right%20to%20vote.

John F. Kennedy Presidential Library and Museum. "Space Program." Accessed September 24, 2022. https://www.jfklibrary.org/learn/about-jfk/jfk-in-history/space-program.

NCC Staff. "On This Dau\y, Rosa Parks Wouldn't Give Up Her Bus Seat." National Constitution Center. December 1, 2022. https://constitutioncenter.org/blog/it-was-on-this-day-that-rosa-parks-made-history-by-riding-a-bus#:~:text=Today%20marks%20the%20anniversary%20of,bus%20to%20a%20white%20passenger.

Selverstone, Marc J. "John F. Kennedy: Campaigns and Elections." Miller Center of Public Affairs, University of Virginia. Accessed September 24, 2022. https://millercenter.org/president/kennedy/campaigns-and-elections.

Selverstone, Marc J. "John F. Kennedy: Death of a President." Miller Center of Public Affairs, University of Virginia. Accessed September 24, 2022. https://millercenter.org/president/kennedy/death-of-the-president.

Selverstone, Marc J. "John F. Kennedy: Domestic Affairs." Miller Center of Public Affairs, University of Virginia. Accessed September 24, 2022. https://millercenter.org/president/kennedy/domestic-affairs.

Selverstone, Marc J. "John F. Kennedy: Impact and Legacy." Miller Center of Public Affairs, University of Virginia. Accessed September 24, 2022. https://millercenter.org/president/kennedy/impact-and-legacy.

Selverstone, Marc J. "John F. Kennedy: Life Before the Presidency." Miller Center of Public Affairs, University of Virginia. Accessed September 24, 2022. https://millercenter.org/president/kennedy/life-before-the-presidency.

Lyndon B. Johnson

Germany, Kent. "Lyndon B. Johnson: Domestic Affairs." Miller Center of Public Affairs, University of Virginia. Accessed September 25, 2022. https://millercenter.org/president/lbjohnson/domestic-affairs.

Germany, Kent. "Lyndon B. Johnson: Foreign Affairs." Miller Center of Public Affairs, University of Virginia. Accessed September 25, 2022. https://millercenter.org/president/lbjohnson/foreign-affairs.

Germany, Kent. "Lyndon B. Johnson: Impact and Legacy." Miller Center of Public Affairs, University of Virginia. Accessed September 25, 2022. https://millercenter.org/president/lbjohnson/impact-and-legacy.

Germany, Kent. "Lyndon B. Johnson: Life Before the Presidency." Miller Center of Public Affairs, University of Virginia. Accessed September 25, 2022. https://millercenter.org/president/lbjohnson/life-before-the-presidency.

Germany, Kent. "Lyndon B. Johnson: The American Franchise." Miller Center of Public Affairs, University of Virginia. Accessed September 25, 2022. https://millercenter.org/president/lbjohnson/the-american-franchise.

White House Historical Association. "President Johnson and Civil Rights." Accessed September 25, 2022. https://www.whitehousehistory.org/president-johnson-and-civil-rights.

Richard M. Nixon

Foundation News. "Edward Nixon, Brother of President Nixon, Dies at 88." Richard Nixon Foundation. February 27, 2019. https://www.nixonfoundation.org/2019/02/edward-nixon-brother-president-nixon-dies-88/.

Huges, Ken. "Richard Nixon: Domestic Affairs." Miller Center of Public Affairs, University of Virginia. Accessed September 26, 2022. https://millercenter.org/president/nixon/domestic-affairs.

Huges, Ken. "Richard Nixon: Foreign Affairs." Miller Center of Public Affairs, University of Virginia. Accessed September 26, 2022. https://millercenter.org/president/nixon/foreign-affairs.

Huges, Ken. "Richard Nixon: Impact and Legacy." Miller Center of Public Affairs, University of Virginia. Accessed September 26, 2022. https://millercenter.org/president/nixon/impact-and-legacy.

Huges, Ken. "Richard Nixon: Life Before the Presidency." Miller Center of Public Affairs, University of Virginia. Accessed September 26, 2022. https://millercenter.org/president/nixon/life-before-the-presidency.

King Institue. "Nixon, Richard Milous." Accessed September 26, 2022, https://kinginstitute.stanford.edu/encyclopedia/nixon-richard-milhous.

Martin, Nick. "Indian Country Deserves a Better Hero Than Richard Nixon." New Republic. October 21, 2019. https://newrepublic.com/article/155440/indian-country-deserves-better-hero-richard-nixon.

Rosenburg, Jennifer. "Biography of Richard Nixon, 37th President of the United States. ThoughtCo. Last modified May 19, 2019. https://www.thoughtco.com/richard-nixon-fast-facts-104880.

Gerald R. Ford

Gonyea, Don. "The Civil Rights Stand of a Young Gerald Ford." NPR, All Things Considered. July 14, 2013. https://www.npr.org/2013/07/14/201946977/the-civil-rights-stand-of-a-young-gerald-ford.

Greene, John Robert. "Gerald Ford: Domestic Affairs." Miller Center of Public Affairs, University of Virginia. Accessed September 27, 2022. https://millercenter.org/president/ford/domestic-affairs.

Greene, John Robert. "Gerald Ford: Foreign Affairs." Miller Center of Public Affairs, University of Virginia. Accessed September 27, 2022. https://millercenter.org/president/ford/foreign-affairs.

Greene, John Robert. "Gerald Ford: Impact and Legacy." Miller Center of Public Affairs, University of Virginia. Accessed September 27, 2022. https://millercenter.org/president/ford/impact-and-legacy.

Greene, John Robert. "Gerald Ford: Life Before the Presidency." Miller Center of Public Affairs, University of Virginia. Accessed September 27, 2022. https://millercenter.org/president/ford/life-before-the-presidency.

James E. Carter

Barrow, Bill. "Jimmy Carter, Trounced in 1980, Gets a Fresh Look from History." Apnews. August 19, 2021. https://apnews.com/article/lifestyle-middle-east-jimmy-carter-18eab7024282910f6aab29026a1e04e2.

Strong, Robert A. "Jimmy Carter: Domestic Affairs." Miller Center of Public Affairs, University of Virginia. Accessed September 28, 2022. https://millercenter.org/president/carter/domestic-affairs.

Strong, Robert A. "Jimmy Carter: Foreign Affairs." Miller Center of Public Affairs, University of Virginia. Accessed September 28, 2022. https://millercenter.org/president/carter/foreign-affairs.

Strong, Robert A. "Jimmy Carter: Impact and Legacy." Miller Center of Public Affairs, University of Virginia. Accessed September 28, 2022. https://millercenter.org/president/carter/impact-and-legacy.

Strong, Robert A. "Jimmy Carter: Life Before the Presidency." Miller Center of Public Affairs, University of Virginia. Accessed September 28, 2022. https://millercenter.org/president/carter/life-before-the-presidency.

Woodruf, Judy and Alter, Jonothan. "Why Jimmy Carter May Be the Most Misunderstood President in American History." PBS News Hour. April 7, 2021. https://www.pbs.org/newshour/show/why-jimmy-carter-may-be-the-most-misunderstood-president-in-american-history.

Ronald Reagan

Cannon, Lou. "Ronald Reagan: Domestic Affairs." Miller Center of Public Affairs, University of Virginia. Accessed October 1, 2022. https://millercenter.org/president/reagan/domestic-affairs.

Cannon, Lou. "Ronald Reagan: Impact and Legacy." Miller Center of Public Affairs, University of Virginia. Accessed October 1, 2022. https://millercenter.org/president/reagan/impact-and-legacy.

Cannon, Lou. "Ronald Reagan: Life Before the Presidency." Miller Center of Public Affairs, University of Virginia. Accessed October 1, 2022. https://millercenter.org/president/reagan/life-before-the-presidency.

Kenton, Will. "Trickle-Down Economics. Theory, Policies, Critique." Investopedia. Last modified August 24, 2022. https://www.investopedia.com/terms/t/trickledowntheory.asp.

Martin Michel, Chavez, Linda, and Fauntroy, Michael. "Remembering President Reagan's Civil Rights Legacy." NPR, Tell Me More. February 4, 2011. https://www.npr.org/2011/02/04/133497430/Remembering-Presidents-Reagan-Civil-Rights-Legacy.

Robinson, Peter. "Tear Down This Wall:' How Top Advisors Opposed Reagan's Challenge to Gorbachev—But Lost." National Archives. Summer, 2007. https://www.archives.gov/publications/prologue/2007/summer/berlin.html.

The Governors' Gallery. "Ronald Reagan." Accessed October 1, 2022. https://governors.library.ca.gov/33-reagan.html.

The Investopedia Team. "Full Employment: Definition, Types, and Examples." Investopedia. Last modified February 3, 2023. https://www.investopedia.com/terms/f/fullemployment.asp.

George H. W. Bush

Haines, Errin. "What Was George H. W. Bush' Record on Race?" PBS News Hour. December 4, 2018. https://www.pbs.org/newshour/politics/what-was-george-h-w-bushs-record-on-race.

Knott, Stephen. "George H. W. Bush: Domestic Affairs." Miller Center of Public Affairs, University of Virginia. Accessed October 3, 2022. https://millercenter.org/president/bush/domestic-affairs.

Knott, Stephen. "George H. W. Bush: Foreign Affairs." Miller Center of Public Affairs, University of Virginia. Accessed October 3, 2022. https://millercenter.org/president/bush/foreign-affairs.

Knott, Stephen. "George H. W. Bush: Impact and Legacy." Miller Center of Public Affairs, University of Virginia. Accessed October 3, 2022. https://millercenter.org/president/bush/impact-and-legacy.

Knott, Stephen. "George H. W. Bush: Life Before the Presidency." Miller Center of Public Affairs, University of Virginia. Accessed October 3, 2022. https://millercenter.org/president/bush/life-before-the-presidency.

William Jefferson Clinton

International Trade Administration. "North American Free Trade Agreement." Accessed October 5, 2022. https://www.trade.gov/north-american-free-trade-agreement-nafta.

National Parks Service. "President William Jefferson Clinton." Accessed October 5, 2022. https://www.nps.gov/features/malu/feat0002/wof/William_Clinton.htm.

Riley, Russell L. "Bill Clinton: Impact and Legacy." Miller Center of Public Affairs, University of Virginia. Accessed October 5, 2022. https://millercenter.org/president/clinton/impact-and-legacy.

Riley, Russell L. "Bill Clinton: Life Before the Presidency." Miller Center of Public Affairs, University of Virginia. Accessed October 5, 2022. https://millercenter.org/president/clinton/life-before-the-presidency.

The Editors of Encyclopedia Britannica. "Hope, Arkansas, United States." Encyclopedia Britannica. Last modified April 16, 2018. https://www.britannica.com/place/Hope-Arkansas/additional-info#history.

George W. Bush

Bush, George W. "Remarks by President George W. Bush at the Civil Rights Summit." George W. Bush Presidential Center. April 11, 2014. https://www.bushcenter.org/publications/remarks-by-president-george-w-bush-at-the-civil-rights-summit.

Gregg, Gary L II. "George W. Bush: Domestic Affairs." Miller Center of Public Affairs, University of Virginia. Accessed October 6, 2022. https://millercenter.org/president/gwbush/domestic-affairs.

Gregg, Gary L II. "George W. Bush: Foreign Affairs." Miller Center of Public Affairs, University of Virginia. Accessed October 6, 2022. https://millercenter.org/president/gwbush/foreign-affairs.

Gregg, Gary L II. "George W. Bush: Impact and Legacy." Miller Center of Public Affairs, University of Virginia. Accessed October 6, 2022. https://millercenter.org/president/gwbush/impact-and-legacy.

Gregg, Gary L II. "George W. Bush: Life Before the Presidency." Miller Center of Public Affairs, University of Virginia. Accessed October 6, 2022. https://millercenter.org/president/gwbush/life-before-the-presidency.

Barrack Obama

Bryant, Nick. "Barrack Obama Legacy: Did he Improve US Race Relations?" BBC News. January 10, 2017. https://www.bbc.com/news/world-us-canada-38536668.

Nelson, Michael. "Barrack Obama: Domestic Affairs." Miller Center of Public Affairs, University of Virginia. Accessed October 7, 2022. https://millercenter.org/president/obama/domestic-affairs.

Nelson, Michael. "Barrack Obama: Foreign Affairs." Miller Center of Public Affairs, University of Virginia. Accessed October 7, 2022. https://millercenter.org/president/obama/foreign-affairs.

Nelson, Michael. "Barrack Obama: Impact and Legacy." Miller Center of Public Affairs, University of Virginia. Accessed October 7, 2022. https://millercenter.org/president/obama/impact-and-legacy.

Nelson, Michael. "Barrack Obama: Life Before the Presidency." Miller Center of Public Affairs, University of Virginia. Accessed October 7, 2022. https://millercenter.org/president/obama/life-before-the-presidency.

Donald J. Trump

Howard, Terry and Clearinghouse." Case: United States v. Fred C. Trump, Donald Trump, and Trump Management, Inc." Civil Rights Litigation Clearinghouse. Last modified December 15, 2022. https://clearinghouse.net/case/15342/.

Waterhouse, Benjamin C. "Donald Trump: Domestic Affairs." Miller Center of Public Affairs, University of Virginia. Accessed October 8, 2022. https://millercenter.org/president/trump/domestic-affairs.

Waterhouse, Benjamin C. "Donald Trump: Impact and Legacy." Miller Center of Public Affairs, University of Virginia. Accessed October 8, 2022. https://millercenter.org/donald-trump-impact-and-legacy.

Waterhouse, Benjamin C. "Donald Trump: Life Before the Presidency." Miller Center of Public Affairs, University of Virginia. Accessed October 8, 2022. https://millercenter.org/president/trump/life-presidency.